Respor

David Sparks

Responsive Prayers

FOR EVERY WEEK OF THE CHURCH YEAR

YEAR

C

REVISED COMMON
LECTIONARY

WOOD LAKE

Editor: Mike Schwartzentruber
Proofreader: Pattie Bender
Designer: Robert MacDonald

Library and Archives Canada Cataloguing in Publication
Sparks, David, 1938-, author
Responsive prayers : for every week of the church year, year C, revised common
lectionary / David Sparks. Includes index.
Issued in print and electronic formats.
ISBN 978-1-77343-031-7 (softcover). – ISBN 978-1-77343-141-3(HTML)
1. Pastoral prayers. 2. Church year – Prayer-books and devotions—
English. I. Title.
BV250.S65 2018   264'.13   C2018-902095-4   C2018-902096-2

Published by Wood Lake Publishing Inc.
485 Beaver Lake Road, Kelowna, BC, Canada, V4V 1S5
www.woodlake.com | 250.766.2778

Wood Lake Publishing acknowledges the financial support of the Government of
Canada. Wood Lake Publishing acknowledges the financial support of the Province of
British Columbia through the Book Publishing Tax Credit.

Wood Lake Publishing would like to acknowledge that we operate in the unceded
territory of the Syilx/Okanagan peoples, and we work to support reconciliation and
challenge the legacies of colonialism. The Syilx/Okanagan territory is a diverse and
beautiful landscape of deserts and lakes, alpine forests and endangered grasslands.
We honour the ancestral stewardship of the Syilx/Okanagan people.

Printed in Canada. Printing 10 9 8 7 6 5 4 3 2 1

Contents

Gratitudes

My thanks to all at Wood Lake Publishing who have been involved in this "responsive" follow up to the *Prayers to Share* and *Pastoral Prayers to Share* series of books.

I am especially grateful to Mike Schwartzentruber for gracefully shaping the format, words, and content of this *Lectionary Year C* book of prayers. It is a more faithful and a more practical liturgical resource because of his efforts.

Thanks also to Robert MacDonald for his eye-catching cover design and effective layout of the book.

Thanks to my wife, Kathy, for her patient and loving support even when I have been "somewhere away in the clouds" focussed on this writing project.

And to the members of congregations where I have led worship, my wholehearted thanks. Your concerns, your needs, your reflections on the way life is and how it might be have all found a place in these pages. I couldn't have written this book without you!

Introduction

My grateful thanks to the many worship leaders who found the *Prayers to Share* and the *Pastoral Prayers to Share* series helpful. It has been humbling to receive your thanks and it is wonderful to have this opportunity to share another set of lectionary-based responsive prayers with you.

The cornerstone or foundation block of this new prayer book for Year C (2018, 2021, 2024, 2027...), and for the other books to come in this series, continues to be that public prayer is not just the exclusive preserve of the worship leader, but a dynamic and responsive act faithfully involving both leader and people. We are all involved in this essential part of the service – praying to God together!

In the previous series, I stressed the value of a thematic format for the service so that, based on the scripture readings, prayers and songs or hymns all have a common theme running through them. In practice, this meant that the gospel reading was dominant. In this volume, *Responsive Prayers, Year C*, I have used readings other than the gospel reading to form the basis or the starting point of many prayers. This will give the worship leader more scope to match the prayer to a variety of themes.

At the end of the day, it is the worship leader for a given Sunday who creates the prayer. My hope is that the prayers within these pages will be changed, added to, or simply used as inspiration or as a focus point by the worship leader. Purchase of this book automatically includes the right to adapt and use the prayers in this way within the congregation, without seeking any additional permission. If you are the worship leader, the prayer – whether it is an opening prayer, an affirmation, an offering or a pastoral prayer – is your prayer for that congregation for that day. It is the worship leader's words together with the words of the congregation that will bring thanks and praise to God.

You will find in many of the prayers a "time of silent reflection." This quiet time features especially in the confessional or theme prayer and is a reminder of the value of a space where congregational members can offer their own thoughts and feelings to God without other people's words getting in the way. As a worship leader, I encourage you to look for spaces where the congregation can pray their own prayers, or include a time of silence as part of the common prayer time.

The huge scope of the Internet resources and the use of PowerPoint and a screen makes it possible for the worship leader to engage the senses of congregants in ways never possible before. Images – which can be found in and chosen from vast online picture archives – can sometimes say more than the most expressive words. You can talk about a thundering waterfall, but it is much more effective to show a still image or moving picture of the cascading torrent. Using Internet music sources, you can fit music to the theme or mood of the prayer. Mind you, it is sometimes difficult to find a form of music that will work with all congregants. Will jazz be the common denominator, or blues, or classical, or meditation music, or nature sounds, or…? Younger members of the congregation can often give assistance if you are struggling to find and fit appropriate music and pictures to your prayer or service theme.

"What does God require of us," as worship leaders? Only that we engage ourselves wholeheartedly in bringing praise and glory to God, and that we are about the active prayers of doing justice, loving kindness, and walking humbly with the Holy One.

Call to Worship, Opening Prayer

Although there is a Call and Opening Prayer included for each week, you will find that often you will be able to use the Call to Worship as the Opening Prayer with only minor changes.

Prayers of confession

There is a trend in many churches to leave out the prayer of confession altogether. The largely unexpressed feeling is that "confessing sins" is an outdated concept and makes the congregation feel uneasy. "Better not to bother with it, and anyway, no one will notice."

My sense is that this is a reaction to the heavy-handed "miserable offender" prayers of a generation ago. No one wants to be beaten over the head with their shortcomings. This book still includes some prayers of confession, both individual and collective, but I have broadened the scope to include affirmations and prayers that are thematic. Included in each set of prayers is an "assurance," which sometimes is an assurance of pardon but more often is an assurance of God's way or God's compassion.

I hope you will think carefully before abandoning a second prayer before the scripture reading, and use the opportunity to allow holy space for congregants to listen for God's voice, and to offer their own silent prayers.

Pastoral prayer pattern

Those who have used the *Pastoral Prayers to Share* series will be familiar with the four divisions that form the prayer.

Prayers for the world, including prayers for persons or groups of persons in the local town, city, or municipality, and the neighbourhood.

Prayers for the suffering, including prayers for those who have suffered loss, those who are sick, those who are caregivers, the bereaved, and those who support them.

Prayers for the church/faith community, the local church, wider church groupings, and faith communities supported by mission money throughout the world.

Prayers for ourselves acknowledging the fact that persons worshipping have specific needs and want these to be recognized in worship.

Rather than a full pastoral prayer, this volume, and the other volumes in this series, includes a "pastoral prayer pattern" that gives suggestions for the content of two of the four sections, and a common bidding and response that may be used at the beginning and end of all four sections.

Pastoral praying: getting God to do the hard work?

In most faith communities, the pastoral prayer is the sole responsibility of the worship leader.

The worship leader writes the prayer or chooses the prayer to be used and then delivers it with the hope that congregational members will silently make the prayer theirs as well.

Usually the prayer consists of a series petitions to God pointing out where assistance is needed to bring change, with the implicit hope that the Holy Spirit will come and make the necessary changes: for example, "Be with those in our congregation who are sick. Grant them endurance in the midst of pain and hope when there seems to be no end to suffering."

Does God work like this? Does God listen for the prayers and then send the Holy Spirit to put things right? If you listen to many pastoral prayers on Sunday morning, you would be forgiven for thinking that this is exactly the way we expect God to work. The trouble is that when peace doesn't come in the Middle East or when cancer persists or gets worse despite our prayers, the Holy Spirit seems impotent. "We prayed, but nothing changed; our prayers were a waste of breath," is a typical angry response.

These prayer leaders present an image of a divine being who stands ready to intervene on the side of whatever the leader considers right. But this is a personal judgement. Does God stand with the Israelis or the Palestinians in the Middle East conflict? For the person suffering with cancer, the most compassionate outcome may be that he or she dies and does not suffer anymore. What sort of image of the divine would be helpful here? Not an interventionist miracle worker, but a Holy One who stands with those who suffer, and who encourages compassion in the midst of pain and suffering.

What is not made explicit in many of the prayers is that those who listen are challenged to come to the aid of the suffering, and by their words or actions help put an end to the pain. Responding in this way is tough and requires hard work; it is much easier to let God get on with solving the problem. God is so much smarter than we are after all!

In his book *The Use of Praying,* J. Neville Ward puts the concept very well when he says that our (pastoral) prayers are, "A piece of work involving costly self-surrender for God, for the work God wants done on other souls." So the key question is, "What are *we* able to do to ensure our prayers have a good and practical outcome?" Can we stay beside a person who is in a testing situation? Can we write to our elected representative to suggest a government initiative for peace or to end discrimination? Can we suggest a recycle policy for our workplace?

The dangers of naming persons and situations
(* indicates that this is not the person's real name)

A highly emotional congregant came up to the worship leader just before the service started. "Can you pray for Helen Graham's* family? Her mother died last evening." The worship leader dutifully responded by including the request in the "prayers for the bereaved" section: "We pray for Helen Graham's family after the death of her mother June." The problem was that June, though close to death, was still living and continued to live. The worship leader had some explaining to do at next week's service.

In another church, the practice was to ask congregational members to voice their own prayers for those who were sick. A young woman prayed for Sarah Smith,* who was "to go through a series of tests for cancer in the coming week." There was no way of knowing whether Sarah had told her family whether she was going for the tests, or whether Sarah had given permission to be prayed for at this service. Very likely she had not. The repercussions in this situation are not known and the person who said the prayer was likely not aware that every congregational member would be asking themselves, "Do I know that family?" Others would be wondering, "Should I give Sarah a call and let her know I'm thinking about her?"

The worship leader is faced with a dilemma when approaching pastoral prayers. Does she keep the prayers general when dealing issues related to congregational members, or does he name people and situations? Or are there other ways to pray by name for individuals who are sick or who have been bereaved, and yet preserve confidentiality?

Of course, confidentiality isn't an issue if the person who is sick or dying *asks* to be mentioned in the prayers of Sunday morning, or if the worship leader (often the minister) seeks and receives permission to name the person in the service. In either situation, the request can be granted without any hesitation.

If the request to pray for someone by name is received second-hand, then the worship leader should ascertain for herself if this represents the will of the sick or dying person. If it does not, or if the worship leader cannot be sure, he should decline the request and give the reason as confidentiality.

In many congregations, a prayer list is gathered before the service. If only the given name of the person is provided, then there is no problem of including those names in the "sick, suffering and bereaved" sections of the pastoral prayer.

Often there is a space in the pastoral prayer for congregational members to voice the names of persons they are concerned about. Again, if the first name only is used, and the reason for the prayer is *not* given, this is perfectly acceptable. In other words, it's okay if no reason is given and no last name is used.

Another practice is to invite people to light tea lights that have been placed around a central Christ candle *before* the service begins. Then, during the pastoral prayer, reference can simply be made to those "for whom candles have been lit."

It is a natural response to offer to God the name of a loved one who is going through a time of suffering. You want the Holy One to know that your cherished aunt has been diagnosed with cancer, that your grandchild is being bullied, that your best friend's marriage is in turmoil, that you are afraid of what the next visit to the doctor will bring. You do this not demanding a cure or ready to trade relief for church attendance, but simply in the way you would confide a deep trouble to a best friend. There is huge relief in the act of sharing.

There is a need for congregational education around pastoral praying, and this can be achieved through a bulletin or newsletter item, or on your church Facebook page, or as a part of a sermon, or through a series of small group sessions. A combination of some or all these methods is probably the best way to go.

Prayers before the scriptures readings, prayers before the meditation or sermon

For some worship leaders, a prayer before the scriptures and a prayer before the meditation are essential; for others these prayers are optional. In this book, we have provided a number of examples of each at the end of the collection.

Lines in italics

In some of the prayers, certain lines are printed in italics. These may be omitted from the prayer if they are not appropriate to your context.

A final word

Each of you has a prayer voice, a unique way of expressing yourself in prayer before the Holy One. My hope and my prayer is that as a result of using this book you will have the confidence to write your own prayers on a regular basis and find a way of sharing them with other worship leaders.

Advent 1

Jeremiah 33:14–16
Psalm 25:1–10
1 Thessalonians 3:9–13
Luke 21:25–36

A new age is coming very soon... hope rules supreme

Call to Worship *(from 1 Thess. 3:9–13)*

ONE: Give thanks to God.

ALL: **Joy is ours, for Advent has arrived.**

ONE: Give thanks to God.

ALL: **The way ahead will be a holy way.**

ONE: Give thanks to God.

ALL: **Our love for one another will grow strong.**

ONE: Give thanks to God.

ALL: **A baby born to humble parents is at the centre of our time together.**

or

ONE: Watch for the signs, the holy time is near;

ALL: **the time of sharing with those who have least.**

ONE: Watch for the signs, the holy time is near;

ALL: **the time to leave grudges and hurts in the past.**

ONE: Watch for the signs, the holy time is near;

ALL: **the time to ask a question, "Who is my neighbour?"**

ONE: Watch for the signs, the holy time is near;

ALL: **to see Love's face smiling in a little child.**

Opening Prayer

ALL: **Living God, you call us to be hopeful.**

ONE: Watch hopefully; God's realm will become reality,

ALL: **a realm of justice and peace.**

ONE: Watch hopefully; God's way will be followed,

ALL: **the way of empathy and compassion.**

ONE: Watch hopefully; God's Spirit will go to work

ALL: **and the change in attitude and enthusiasm will astound us.**

ONE: Watch hopefully and you will have the strength you need.

ALL: **God will be our friend, our helper, and our guide. Amen.**

or

ONE: Loving God, prepare us for the coming of Jesus.

ALL: **We prepare as we consider our spiritual life-path.**

ONE: Enable us to make good choices for the coming of Jesus.

ALL: **We will make your priorities our priorities, loving God.**

ONE: Bring us together as we prepare for the coming of Jesus.

ALL: **Challenge and enliven us as a faith community.**

ONE: May compassion be our watchword as we prepare for the coming of Jesus,

ALL: **that those among us who are downtrodden and depressed will receive the support and encouragement they need. Amen.**

Advent Prayer of Readiness

ONE: You call us to be watchful and ready, Holy One,

ALL: **to speak out against those who say, "Tomorrow will do."**

ONE: You call us to be ready, Holy One,

ALL: **to expose those who ignore the oppressed and who practice discrimination.**

ONE: You call us to be ready, Holy One,

ALL: **to align ourselves with those who counter apathy with action.**

ONE: You call us to be ready, Holy One,

ALL: **to make clear our discipleship of Jesus, in what we say and what we do.**

ONE: You call us to be watchful and ready, always watchful and ready. *(time of reflection)*

Words of Assurance

ONE: As you put apathy behind you, as you are ready to act,

ALL: **we prepare ourselves for the coming of Jesus.**
Advent readiness is ours. Thanks be to God. Amen.

Offering Prayer

ONE: Wonderful things happen through your gifts.

ALL: **The lonely receive companionship.**
The sick know support.
The displaced find a home.
The persecuted know they are not alone.
Children sing and laugh as they play.

ONE: They are blessed, and we are blessed. Amen.

 ## Pastoral Prayer Pattern *(from Isaiah 2:1–4)*

ONE: Where God's way prevails,

ALL: **people will search for the highest good.**

ONE: *National leaders will strive to help the poorest and those at risk.*
We pray for those addicted to opioids, those who sleep on the street in our city because no one will rent them rooms.
Peace will be a priority.
Money spent on guns and bombs will be redirected to help people training for useful work.
We pray for those who advocate for a change in national priorities.
Education will be the right of each person.
Barriers of racial background, gender, or economic status will be broken down.

We pray for those who are struggling to reach their learning potential.

This is our Advent hope: where God's way prevails,

ALL: **people will search for the highest good.**

ONE: Where God's way prevails,

ALL: **the suffering will know relief.**

ONE: Introverts will know a quiet place.

Extroverts will find company.

People in pain will find understanding.

People challenged physically will get access to restaurants and washrooms.

People challenged mentally will receive the recognition and resources they need.

We will stay beside family, friends and church family members who are sick. *(time of reflection)*

Where God's way prevails,

ALL: **the suffering will know relief.**

Commissioning

ONE: The joys and challenges of Advent lie ahead of you.

ALL: **We will meditate carefully.**

We will sing out joyfully.

We will share generously.

We will stay beside the downhearted with compassion.

We will face the powerful, directly.

ONE: And with open arms, we welcome Jesus, born to Mary at Bethlehem.

Advent 2

Malachi 3:1–4
     or Baruch 5:1–9
Luke 1:68–79
Philippians 1:3–11
Luke 3:1–6

Malachi prophesies the coming of the messenger... John preaches and baptizes

Call to Worship

ONE: Rejoice! The one who saves is coming:
ALL: **long promised, long awaited;**
ONE: foretold by the prophets;
ALL: **counterpoint to selfishness and evil;**
ONE: the one who drives out fear;
ALL: **the one who frees from oppression.**
ONE: God's merciful presence is known in this saviour:
ALL: **light in the darkness, peace in the conflict.**
We will welcome Jesus, the Christ.

Opening Prayer

ONE: John was called to a ministry in his time and in his place.
John, the prophet, spoke out fearlessly.
ALL: **We are called to speak honestly and truthfully.**
ONE: John baptized without discrimination.
ALL: **We are called to regard all people without concern for race, gender, or economic status.**
ONE: John offered the absolute forgiveness of God.
ALL: **We are called to forgive without reserve.**
ONE: John welcomed Jesus wholeheartedly.
ALL: **We are called to be the friends of Jesus for our time and our place. Amen.**

A Prayer from the Words of the Prophet Isaiah
(from Luke 3:4–6)

ONE: The voice of one crying out in the wilderness.

ALL: **Be with us, loving God, when we feel most alone.** *(time of silent reflection)*

ONE: Prepare the way of the Lord. Make God's paths straight.

ALL: **Be with us, loving God, as we speak out for our faith community when it seems no one is listening.** *(time of silent reflection)*

ONE: Every valley shall be filled and every mountain and hill shall be made low.

ALL: **Be with us, loving God, as we work to bring justice to those who lack a friendly affirmative voice.** *(time of silent reflection)*

ONE: And all humankind will see God's salvation.

ALL: **Be with us, compassionate God, as we work peacefully and patiently to create the community and the world that you would love to see.** *(time of silent reflection)*

Words of Assurance (Peace)

ONE: Peace comes as we reflect on your abundant grace, loving God.

ALL: **Peace comes as we do the work you want us to do.**

ONE: God will give you the resources; God will enable you to take the time you need.

ALL: **Thanks be to God. Amen.**

Offering Prayer

ONE: With these our gifts of money, together with our talents and our time, we offer to bring peace: peace where there is loneliness,

ALL: **the peace of friendship;**

ONE: peace where there is conflict,

ALL: **the peace of reconciliation;**

ONE: peace where there is inaction,

ALL: **the peace of a definite start;**

ONE: peace where there is mindless routine,

ALL: **the peace of fresh vision;**

ONE: the creative peace of Advent,

ALL: **the coming of Jesus, God's chosen one. Amen.**

Pastoral Prayer Pattern

ONE: The time of waiting is over.

ALL: **The messenger will prepare us for God's promised one.**

ONE: We will prepare with joyful worship.
        We will prepare by studying the Word in faith community.
        We will prepare by sharing gifts in our neighbourhood...
        We will prepare by helping those whose names we will never know.
        The time of waiting is over.

ALL: **The messenger will prepare us for God's promised one.**

ONE: The time of waiting is over.

ALL: **The messenger will prepare us for God's promised one.**

ONE: Are you ready to make the necessary changes?
        Will you put apathy behind you?
        Will you leave what is past in the past?
        Will you look to the crying needs of our local community and our world?
        Will you put your faith first? *(time of silence)*
        The time of waiting is over.

ALL: **The messenger will prepare us for God's promised one.**

Commissioning

ONE: Go from here as God's Advent people, ready to be prophets for your time and generation,

ALL: **prepared to take part in God's saving work,**

ONE: ready to speak out against oppression and injustice,

ALL: **prepared to go against selfishness and fear,**

ONE: ready to be a voice for the voiceless,

ALL: **prepared to be an advocate for those who are at risk,**

ONE: ready to speak of Jesus Christ in an unbelieving world,

ALL: **prepared to live out our belief in action.**

ONE: God goes with you. God will strengthen you; there is nothing to fear.

ALL: **Thanks be to God.**

Advent 3

Zephaniah 3:14–20
Isaiah 12:2–6
Philippians 4:4–7
Luke 3:7–18

John the baptizer speaks of radical change

Call to Worship

ONE: Come to this service with joy.

ALL: **We rejoice in this time of prayer and praise, silence, listening, and determination.**

ONE: Come to this service with joy.

ALL: **We rejoice that we can hear and reflect on the life-giving Word, in the Hebrew and Christian scriptures.**

ONE: Come to this service with joy.

ALL: **We rejoice that we can learn and share with our faith community friends.**

ONE: Come to this service with joy.

ALL: **We rejoice that we are strengthened to change our ways and serve together.**

Opening Prayer

ONE: Come singing to God.

ALL: **Words and music combine in heartfelt praise.**

ONE: Come with thanks to God.

ALL: **God's gifts and blessings are myriad and wonderful.**

ONE: Come with sharing to God.

ALL: **We will share our time, we will share our talent.**

ONE: Come humbly, come quietly before God.

ALL: **What does the Lord require of us – in worship and in our life's journey?** *(time of silent reflection)*

ONE: It is a good question. Have we good answers?

ALL: **Amen.**

or

Opening Prayer *(from Philippians 4:4–7)*

ONE: Rejoice in God always, and again we say, "Rejoice!"

ALL: **Rejoice in God, our Creator; the skies, the seas, the variety of humankind – all of it is wonder-full.**

ONE: Rejoice in God always and again we say, "Rejoice!"

ALL: **Rejoice in God, source of compassion; the despised and vulnerable receive hope.**

ONE: Rejoice in God always and again we say, "Rejoice!"

ALL: **Rejoice in God. In God's realm, justice and forgiveness are the watchwords.**

ONE: Rejoice in God always and again we say, "Rejoice!"

ALL: **Rejoice in God, anointer of Jesus, in whom the eternal values are clear. Rejoice in God always and again we say, "Rejoice!" Amen.**

A Prayer Inviting Change *(from Luke:3 10–14)*

ONE: John says, "Do those things that show you have changed your life around."

ALL: **We are ready to move from "the way it's always been done."**

ONE: A good beginning. But are those of you who have money and resources ready to share with those who have little or none?

ALL: **We will find a way to give or to receive according to our situation.**

ONE: What about those of you who have enough to eat, and comfortable homes?

ALL: **We who have plenty will share with those who don't have enough food or a comfortable home, and who believe that nothing will change.**

ONE: And what about those of you in positions of power, people who can influence others?

ALL: **We who are privileged will be fair; we will act justly and with compassion.**

ONE: We hear the voice of John, the prophet, challenging the people of his time and we know that he is speaking to us.

ALL: **Good news for John's time, good news for our time, but some major changes will be needed.** *(time of silent reflection)*

Assurance of a New Way

ONE: Will you consider the way of radical change that John is offering?

ALL: **His challenge is for *our* time and situation as well as his time.**

ONE: Are you ready to walk a new way?

ALL: **We are followers of Jesus Christ. We will humbly follow his selfless, sharing way, and we will care as he cared.**

Offering Prayer

ONE: We give joyfully, generously,

ALL: **for we have seen suffering and sadness near and far, and we want it to end.**

ONE: We give joyfully, generously,

ALL: **for our faith community continues to care for its lonely and isolated ones.**

ONE: We give joyfully, generously,

ALL: **for we want children and adults to learn about Jesus and to hear the gospel story.**

ONE: We give joyfully, generously,

ALL: **for then the homeless person and the refugee will know support.**

ONE: Because we are certain that our gifts will be justly and compassionately used,

ALL: **we give joyfully and generously. Amen.**

Pastoral Prayer Pattern *(from Luke 3:3, 6)*

ONE: Are you ready?

ALL: **We are ready to work for radical change.**

ONE: Radical change, where the voiceless will find their voice and those of us who find it difficult to oppose the powerful will be given strength.
Radical change, where those who are waiting for medical treatment receive it.
Radical change, where those who are in pain get relief.
Radical change, for those who are struggling and for those who are feeling deeply the loss of loved ones.
We bring into our mind's eye and pray silently or out loud for people we know, and for members of our faith community. *(time of silent reflection)*
Are you ready?

ALL: **We are ready to work for radical change.**

ONE: Are you ready?

ALL: **We are ready to work for radical change.**

ONE: In our faith community (church), we will look to the needs of our neighbourhood as carefully as to those of our faith community.
We will provide food and crafts midweek for children, as well as a Sunday celebration.
We will feed the spirits of our members through weekly mediation, study, and prayer.
We will give as much for mission needs as for the local church.
In our faith community (church),

ALL: **we will work for radical change.**

Commissioning

ONE: What will you do as you leave this church?

ALL: **We will offer our thanks joyfully, and our hopes and dreams confidently.**
We will pray for courage hopefully, and we will work selflessly.
We will be prepared to change radically, and we will give bigheartedly.
We will support our neighbour appropriately, and the stranger in need generously.

ONE: As you leave this church, the loving God goes with you.

ALL: **We go forward fearlessly.**

Advent 4

Micah 5:2–5a
Luke 1:47–55
           or Psalm 80:1–7
Hebrews 10:5–10
Luke 1:39–45, (46–55)

Elizabeth recognizes Mary as chosen by God

Call to Worship

ONE: God has remembered us; we are God's people.
ALL: **The love of God embraces us as we worship.**
ONE: God has remembered us that,
ALL: **we bring our thanks and praise to God in return.**
ONE: God has remembered us
ALL: **and calls us to work as God's faithful community.**
ONE: In time and beyond time,
ALL: **God will remember us and cherish us as friends.**

Opening Prayer

ONE: In the coming of Jesus there is hope;
ALL: **the proud will be scattered, the humble will receive their due.**
ONE: In the coming of Jesus there is peace;
ALL: **the peacemakers will be recognized, those who fight will get nowhere.**
ONE: In the coming of Jesus there is joy;
ALL: **the downtrodden will celebrate, the power people will be exposed.**
ONE: In the coming of Jesus there is love;
ALL: **a love without limits, a love that conquers fear and loneliness.**
We rejoice in the coming of Jesus. Amen.

A Magnificat Prayer

ONE: God can do great things, if we work in harmony with God.

ALL: **From generation to generation, God has been with us.**

ONE: If we work in harmony with God,

ALL: **the disadvantaged will get their chance, the proud will be brought low.**

ONE: If we work in harmony with God,

ALL: **the refugee will find a home, the immigrant will be supported.**

ONE: If we work in harmony with God,

ALL: **those who have so much will share and the deprived will get what they need.**

ONE: If we work in harmony with God.
       Abraham was in harmony with God. Jeremiah was in harmony with God. Loving Mary was in harmony with God.
       We seek such harmony of spirit and action. *(time of silence)*

Assurance of a New Way

ONE: We search, loving God, for those aspects of our lives and for those aspects of our faith community that are not in harmony with your will and purpose.

ALL: **You know us through and through.**
       You know that change is possible.
       You will give us the strength of mind and spirit to bring change.

ONE: God's love will win out and you will be renewed.

ALL: **Thanks be to God. Amen.**

Offering Prayer

ONE: As we offer our gifts, loving God, give us the big-hearted attitude of Mary:

ALL: **willing to give graciously,**
       ready to question when necessary,

prepared to share the best of our personal gifts for church community,
certain that God will work in ways we know and in ways we do not yet know.

ONE: You have given faithfully, and the Good News of the coming of Jesus Christ will be proclaimed.

ALL: **Amen.**

 Pastoral Prayer Pattern

ONE: We are waiting, waiting for the Christ-child,

ALL: **remembering the God-given opportunity in Jesus.**

ONE: We are waiting for Jesus the Christ, who spoke out against the powerful, and who today would speak for the oppressed. *We pray for refugees, and for those who suffer for their political views.*
We are waiting for Jesus the Christ, who came to understand that God's compassion knows no barriers of nationality or faith, and who today would work with Buddhists, Muslims, and Hindus. *(current situation)*
We are waiting for Jesus the Christ, who was not prepared to put off proclaiming the values of God's realm, and who today would confront those who pollute the skies and oceans. *(current situation)*
We are waiting for the Christ-child, born into a poor, vulnerable family, and who today would be protesting against the gross inequality of income and opportunity. *(current situation)*

ONE: We are waiting, waiting for the Christ-child,

ALL: **remembering the God-given opportunity in Jesus.**

ONE: We are waiting, waiting for the Christ-child,

ALL: **remembering the God-given opportunity in Jesus.**

ONE: We are waiting for the opportunity to give thanks for God's most gracious gift in Jesus:
waiting for the opportunity to sing with heartfelt

anticipation of the promised one who is coming,
waiting for the opportunity to serve the humblest and
receive from the most affluent,
waiting for the opportunity to work through the gift-
giving and gift-receiving challenges we confront in
Advent.
We are waiting for the Christ-child,

ALL: **remembering the God-given opportunity in Jesus.**

Commissioning

ONE: Go as a faithful community of Jesus Christ,

ALL: **venturing hopefully for the just way,**
seeking peace in the struggle,
serving our fellow Christians with joy,
and embracing the needs of a suffering world with
love.

ONE: Go in the determined and resilient spirit of Jesus.

ALL: **God goes with us, we cannot fail.**
We *will* make a difference.

Christmas Eve/Day

Christmas, Proper 1 (Years A, B, C)

Isaiah 9:2–7
Psalm 96
Titus 2:11–14
Luke 2:1–14, (15–20)

The birth of Jesus

Call to Worship *(slowly and gently prayed)*

ONE: God's chosen child will be born in a stable.

ALL: **We feel the anticipation. We feel the uncertainty of Joseph and Mary. The time for the birth of Jesus has arrived.** *(time of silent reflection)*

ONE: God's chosen child is announced by angels to shepherds on the hillside.

ALL: **We feel the amazement of working shepherds; we feel their fear turning to joy.** *(time of silent reflection)*

ONE: God's chosen child and his parents are visited by the shepherds.

ALL: **We feel the eagerness of the shepherds; we feel their enthusiasm to recount the wonderful story of the angels visit.** *(time of silent reflection)*

ONE: Mary, mother of God's chosen child, reflects on what the shepherds have told her.

ALL: **We feel her challenges as a new mother; we feel her wonder at the events that have surrounded her son's birth.** *(time of silent reflection)*

Opening Prayer

ONE: The time of patient waiting is over! The time of anxiety is over! Jesus is born!

ALL: **The angels rejoice!**

ONE: The long wait foretold by the prophets is over! The time of questioning is over!

ALL: **The angels rejoice, the shepherds rejoice!**

ONE: The time full of hope for humankind has come, a wonder-full time has come!

ALL: **The angels rejoice, the shepherds rejoice, and we rejoice!**

ONE: A time when peace and compassion will be known and practiced, a time yearned for throughout the Earth.

ALL: **The angels rejoice, the shepherds rejoice, and our rejoicing is joined with the generations that came before us, and those yet to be! Amen.**

A Christmas Prayer for Peace

ONE: Loving God, where the fighting is intense in *(name areas of conflict)*,
where children are injured,
where families run for their lives,

ALL: **our prayer is, "Peace."**

ONE: Loving God, where families are separated over the holiday by work, by distance, or by conflict,

ALL: **our prayer is, "Peace."**

ONE: Loving God, where our family members or friends are suffering or depressed at this celebration time, we remember them in the silence of our hearts. *(time of silence)*
Loving God,

ALL: **our prayer is, "Peace."**

ONE: Where church family members are unable to be with us through sickness or infirmity or because they have travelled far from here, loving God,

ALL: **our prayer is, "Peace."**

ONE: And where we are troubled or afraid, unable to forgive or unable to put our concerns into words, *(time of silent reflection)*
loving God,

ALL: **our prayer is, "Peace" – your deep lasting peace, the peace that passes all human understanding. Amen.**

Offering Prayer

ONE: We see a newborn baby secure within a manger; we see the parents, Mary and Joseph, and imagine their hope for the days that lie ahead.

ALL: **Our hearts overflow with thanks for God's wonderful gift.**

ONE: We see the humble shepherds coming to this simple place; we hear their stories of angels and their songs of joy as they return to their work with the flocks. They have received so much.

ALL: **We join in their rejoicing. We too have received so much in the coming of Jesus, God's promised one.**

ONE: Bless these Christmas offerings, loving God.

ALL: **Bless all we have given and all we have received, so that the name of Jesus will be honoured in our homes, and the way of Jesus followed in our lives and world – a way of caring, a way of love. Amen.**

Pastoral Prayer Pattern

ONE: We celebrate the birth of Jesus,

ALL: **our hope for wonderful change.**

One   In the birth of Jesus there is hope for those who are refugees, a safe place for those without a home. *(name contemporary examples)*
There is hope of reunion for those separated from family members, hope of freedom for those under the burden of the powerful. *(name contemporary examples)*
There is hope of food where there is none, for starving children above all. *(name contemporary examples)*
Rejoice from the bottom of your hearts!

ALL: **We are partners in the wonderful change that the birth of Jesus brings.**

ONE: We celebrate the birth of Jesus,
ALL: our hope for wonderful change.
ONE: In the birth of Jesus there is hope for each one of us:
      hope for an end to the accustomed ways that limit us;
      hope for new friends, fresh ventures;
      hope for turning our dreams into reality;
      hope for an end to a sense that we cannot break free.
      Rejoice from the bottom of your hearts!
      We celebrate the birth of Jesus,
ALL: our hope for wonderful change.

Commissioning

ONE: Go from this church celebrating the birth of Jesus
      Christ,
**ALL: welcoming the lonely to our homes with friendship,
      welcoming families to our church with joy,
      welcoming the stranger/refugee to our community
      with generosity,
      welcoming the suffering with compassion,
      welcoming the bereaved with our patient presence,
      welcoming the searcher to our faith community with
      listening,
      welcoming the member of another faith group with
      acceptance.**
ONE: In your spirit of welcoming, the spirit of Christ will live,
ALL: and God's name will be praised.

Christmas Eve/Day

Christmas, Proper 2 (Years A, B, C)

Isaiah 62:6–12
Psalm 97
Titus 3:4–7
Luke 2:(1–7), 8–20

The birth of Jesus

Call to Worship

ONE: Come to this church with joy.

ALL: **This wonderful day *has arrived/ is so close*, the day of Christ's birth.**

ONE: Come to this church with humility.

ALL: **Our Christmas has been graced with Jesus, God's chosen child.**

ONE: Come to this church to celebrate.

ALL: **Whether family member, friend, or stranger, we welcome one another, and we are blessed.**

ONE: Come to this church and find deep peace

ALL: **in the wrinkled face of a newborn child.**

Opening Prayer

ONE: Your love amazes us, living God.

ALL: **Loves comes to us through a down-to-earth couple and their newborn child.**

ONE: Your love encourages us, living God.

ALL: **Love comes to us as working shepherds are surprised and moved.**

ONE: Your love touches us, living God.

ALL: **Love calls us to reflection, as Mary thought deeply about what the birth of Jesus meant.**

ONE: Your love inspires us, living God.

ALL: Love calls us to see ordinary events in your wonderful
        light. Amen.

A Prayer for Those Who Struggle at Christmas

ONE: Loving God,

ALL: we thank you for the excitement and wonder of family
        home for the holidays.

ONE: We pray for those of us who have no family members
        with whom to share news and presents.

ALL: We thank you for family members who have travelled
        by air, car, and bus to gather around the Christmas
        table. *(time of silent reflection)*

ONE: We pray for those who have to work during this time,
        or who are prevented from coming home by distance
        or by lack of money.

ALL: We thank you for the fun, laughter, and news we share
        at home. *(time of silent reflection)*

ONE: We pray for those of us who are separated from family
        members by hurt, anger, or conflict.

ALL: We thank you for the birth of Jesus to Mary and
        Joseph, the awe-inspiring "reason for the season." *(time
        of silent reflection)*

ONE: We pray for those of who follow Jesus faithfully, for
        those who question their beliefs, and for those for who
        have not yet discovered Christian faith on their
        spiritual journey. *(time of silent reflection)*

Assurance of Peace

ONE: In our joy and in our sadness,

ALL: in our doubt and in our believing,

ONE: in our disappointment and in our good surprises,

ALL: at our endings and at our beginnings,

ONE: you are there for us, loving God.

ALL: Through all the twists and turns of life, and at this
        wonderful time of Christmas, you are there.

ONE: The peace that cannot be shaken,
the peace that cannot be taken away,
the peace that will end conflict.

ALL: **Thank you, Holy One. Amen.**

Offering Prayer

ONE: Transform our gifts at this time of the birth of Jesus Christ, loving God.

ALL: **Accept our money and set it to work for justice and compassion.**
Accept our time and use it to bring freedom and new faith endeavours.
Accept our skills and talents. Use them to ease suffering and to make the truth known.
Accept all that we can give to bring honour to your chosen one, born to humble parents in the town of Bethlehem all those years ago. Amen.

 ## Pastoral Prayer Pattern

ONE: In the spirit of the saviour,

ALL: **what seemed impossible is now possible.**

ONE: Those out of work will renew their efforts to seek work and training.
The depressed and downhearted will detect a glimmer of hope in the darkness.
Those whose medical treatment is delayed will speak again of their needs to their health professional.
Those in pain will put their unspoken fears into words.
Those who have lost loved ones will know the strong support of family and friends.
We pray for those whose tough times go unremembered at this time of joy and celebration.
(time of silence)
In the spirit of the saviour,

ALL: **what seemed impossible is now possible.**

ONE: In the spirit of the saviour,

ALL: **what seemed impossible is now possible.**

ONE: Those doing small but essential jobs will receive the thanks they deserve.

The learning needs of the faith community will be sought out and met.

Partnership with local groups to relieve need will become possible.

An oasis of quiet will be found amidst the noise and hurry.

In the spirit of the saviour,

ALL: **what seemed impossible is now possible.**

Commissioning

ONE: Go from here as those who have joyfully greeted the Christ child.

ALL: **The singing of the angels will echo in our praises.**
The amazement of the shepherds will lift our spirits.
The peace shared in the holy family will bring us the calm we need.
The reflection of Mary will cause us to ponder deeply.
The thanksgiving of the shepherds will be mirrored in our thanks for God's most gracious gift, Jesus the Christ.

Christmas Day

Proper 3 (Years A, B, C)

Isaiah 52:7–10
Psalm 98
Hebrews 1:1–4, (5–12)
John 1:1–14

Our world is God's world

Call to Worship *(from Psalm 98)*

ONE: God is loyal and constantly loves the people of God. You are God's people.

ALL: **We are God's people. We will praise God with songs and shouts of joy.**

ONE: God loves God's world and everything in it.

ALL: **We are God's people and we give thanks for the wonders of creation.**

ONE: If the rivers could joyfully clap their hands they would; if the hills could become a choir they would praise God.

ALL: **For God will save God's people, and in the birth of Jesus salvation is ours, for everyone and for always.**

Opening Prayer *(from John 1:1–9)*

ONE: The light shines in Bethlehem.

ALL: **Jesus is born: the light of Jesus, son of Joseph and Mary,**

ONE: the light foretold by the prophets,

ALL: **made clear by baptizer John beside the Jordan River.**

ONE: The light will overcome the darkest events and people of the world,

ALL: **and show clearly the way ahead.**

ONE: The true light, the life-bringing light:

ALL: we the people of God rejoice that the light of Jesus Christ will inspire us. Amen.

The Word of Life *(from John 1:14)*

ONE: The Word has come to our world; nothing will be the same again.

ALL: **The true Word, the word that brings life.**

ONE: The Word will speak hope to the downtrodden,

ALL: **and will speak freedom to those who are held captive.**

ONE: The Word will work compassionately with the suffering,

ALL: **and stay beside those who have lost a loved one,**

ONE: and bring purpose to those who are drifting,

ALL: **and vision to those who are too tired to lift their eyes.**

ONE: The Word was full of grace and truth in Jesus the Christ,

ALL: **and we bring the Word alive in our day and generation.**
(time of silent reflection)

Assurance of Change

ONE: The birth of Jesus changes everything.

ALL: **We hear the Word and rejoice.**

ONE: The birth of Jesus changes everything.

ALL: **We hear the Word and we go to work.**

ONE: The birth of Jesus changes everything.

ALL: **We hear the Word and receive a blessing.**

ONE: The peace of God is your peace.

ALL: **Amen.**

Offering Prayer

ONE: What can we give so that the Christmas story is told, the carols sung, and the Word of God heard?

ALL: **Our gifts make it possible to celebrate the birth of Jesus.**

ONE: What can we do to bring greetings to those who can no longer come to church and to enable the sick to be visited?

ALL: **Our gifts make it possible to include all people in the Christmas celebrations.**

ONE: What can we offer so that the caring work of the church is carried out at home and overseas?

ALL: **Our mission gifts make it possible for the healing and liberating work of the church to be done.**

ONE: As you give, so many are blessed.

ALL: **As we give, so we receive a blessing. Amen.**

   Pastoral Prayer Pattern *(from John 1:5)*

ONE: The light shining out clearly

ALL: **will overcome the darkness.**

ONE: In the light of Christ, nations will share their resources, unmasked.

In the light of Christ, the lack of opportunity for women and girls will become clear.

In the light of Christ, those who exploit children will be revealed.

In the light of Christ, those who pollute air and water will be exposed.

In the light of Christ, those who oppose politically repressive regimes will do so without danger.

The light shining out clearly

ALL: **will overcome the darkness.**

ONE: The light shining out clearly

ALL: **will overcome the darkness.**

The light will illuminate the poverty and homelessness in our neighbourhood.

The light will meet local needs.

The light will show clearly the needs of those who can no longer attend Sunday worship or support church activities.

The light will reach out a friendly hand to members of other faith groups.

The light shining out clearly will overcome the darkness.

Commissioning

ONE: Give thanks for this day:

ALL: **a day of gifts, surprises, and tokens of love.**

ONE: Give thanks for these people:

ALL: **family and friends, cherished church family members.**

ONE: Give thanks for the Word:

ALL: **the Word of life, a word to nourish, a word to surprise, a word to inspire.**

ONE: Give thanks for Jesus:

ALL: **humble by birth, but the revelation of God's way for humankind.**

ONE: We give God thanks and praise for God's anointed one,

ALL: **who speaks to us today and promises God's eternal love.**

First Sunday after Christmas Day

1 Samuel 2:18–20, 26
Psalm 148
Colossians 3:12–17
Luke 2:41–52

Jesus is in the temple

Call to Worship

ONE: Holy One, we worship you.

ALL: **We worship you in our praise and in our prayers this morning.**

ONE: Holy One, we worship you.

ALL: **We worship you as we listen to the Word read in scripture and carefully considered.**

ONE: Holy One, we worship you.

ALL: **We worship as we serve with thoughtfulness and with compassion.**

ONE: Holy One, we worship you.

ALL: **We worship as we question, and as we express our doubts honestly and openly.**

Opening Prayer

ONE: For good parents and caring grandparents,

ALL: **we give you thanks, loving God.**

ONE: For wise teachers and insightful mentors,

ALL: **we give you thanks, loving God.**

ONE: For loyal friends and good companions,

ALL: **we give you thanks, loving God.**

ONE: For inspired and inspiring members of this church,

ALL: **we give you thanks, loving God.**

ONE: And for Jesus, our light for the way,

ALL: we give you thanks, loving God. Amen.

A Prayer of Learning

ONE: Strengthen within us, living God, the will to learn.

ALL: **Enliven us with the desire to search after new truth.**

ONE: Strengthen within us, living God, the will to discover.

ALL: **Keep us on the move to find new opportunities, new prospects.**

ONE: Strengthen within us the will to grow as disciples of Jesus Christ,

ALL: **never satisfied with what we know, always pioneering in the faith.**

ONE: Strengthen within us the will to reach out to those we meet,

ALL: **ready with a helping hand, a listening ear, and the response of one who cares.** *(time of silent reflection)*

Assurance of a New Way

ONE: You, living God, will give us the strength to learn and to discover, to grow and to care.

ALL: **In those times of apathy and weakness, and when we "go with the flow," you stay with us.**
You are our source of determination; you renew us hour by hour, day by day, and we thank you for the new life you make possible. Amen.

Offering Prayer

ONE: Our gifts will be a source of learning within the faith community and far beyond. We offer them to you, gracious God.

ALL: **Our children will be encouraged to ask questions and our young people challenged to discuss political and moral issues.**

ONE: Our adults will study the Bible and inspired writings, and our seniors will keep on sharing their wisdom.

ALL: **We give so that those whose names we do not know will**

learn and prosper through the projects of our mission
fund.

ONE: Accept our gifts, gracious God,

ALL: **and bless us as we put them to work, in the name and
in the way of Jesus. Amen.**

 Pastoral Prayer Pattern

ONE: Jesus listened. Jesus questioned.

ALL: **Jesus was prepared to act.**

ONE: Some families do not know where their next meal will
come from.

ALL: **By advocacy, by community sharing in food banks, we
can help.**

ONE: Some people live rough; some live in their vehicles.

ALL: **By talking to community leaders, by speaking out for
housing geared to income, we can help.**

ONE: Some mentally challenged people end up in prisons.

ALL: **By demanding programs to get them treatment, by
standing with them, we can help.**

ONE: Some elderly folks cannot speak of their deepest
concerns.

ALL: **By establishing what they need and by being their
voice, we can help.**

ONE: We have our clear example. Jesus listened. Jesus
questioned.

ALL: **Jesus was prepared to act.**

ONE: Jesus listened. Jesus questioned.

ALL: **Jesus was prepared to act.**

ONE: We acknowledge our own need to listen most carefully.
We acknowledge our reluctance to hear an opinion
that goes against our own.
We acknowledge our eagerness to acclaim and support
those who think just like we do.

We need the example of Jesus. Jesus listened. Jesus questioned.

Jesus was prepared to act.

Commissioning

ONE: You are teachers. Teach.

ALL: **We will teach with gentleness. We will teach with wisdom. We will always be open to new truth.**

ONE: You are learners. Learn.

ALL: **We will learn with patience, we will learn by doing, we will learn through asking the simple questions.**

ONE: God will bless you as you teach and as you learn. As teachers and learners, you will be God's blessing to others.

ALL: **Thanks be to our gracious God.**

New Year's Day or Sunday

Ecclesiastes 3:1–13
Psalm 8
Revelation 21:1–6a
Matthew 25:31–46

Caring for the needs of all God's people

Call to Worship *(from Ecclesiastes 3:1–13)*

ONE: A New Year, a fresh opportunity for God's people:

ALL: **a time for birth, a time to die.** *(time of silent reflection)*

ONE: A New Year, a fresh opportunity for God's people:

ALL: **a time to plant and a time for pulling up what is planted.** *(time of silent reflection)*

ONE: A New Year, a fresh opportunity for God's people:

ALL: **a time to break down and a time to build up.** *(time of silent reflection)*

ONE: A New Year, a fresh opportunity for God's people:

ALL: **a time for sorrow and a time for joy.** *(time of silent reflection)*

ONE: A New Year, a fresh opportunity for God's people:

ALL: **a time for mourning and a time for dancing. (time of silence)**

ONE: A New Year, a fresh opportunity for God's people:

ALL: **a time to embrace and a time to refrain from embracing.** *(time of silent reflection)*

ONE: A New Year, a fresh opportunity for God's people:

ALL: **a time for finding and a time for losing.** *(time of silent reflection)*

ONE: A New Year, a fresh opportunity for God's people:

ALL: **a time for silence and a time to talk.** *(time of silent reflection)*

ONE: A New Year, a fresh opportunity for God's people:

ALL: **a time for war and a time for peace.** *(time of silent reflection)*

The worship leader can choose from these and other verses in Ecclesiastes 3:1–13. The call may be unhurried. Let congregants go to work in the silence. What is it that I need to bring to birth in my life and what needs to die? What makes me sorrowful and what fills me with joy?

Opening Prayer *(from Psalm 8, which might be read at this point in the service)*

ONE: In this New Year you have work for us to do, living God.

ALL: **We look at the wonders of your creation; we sit awestruck under the stars.**

ONE: We thank you for the limitless universe, for our life within it, and we thank you for our small and wonderful planet.

ALL: **We realize that the health of planet Earth depends on the actions of all humankind. The birds of the air, the fish of the seas, wild flowers, domestic cattle and pets, depend on how we treat the environment.**

ONE: You have given us the power and the resources to keep the air and water pure.
You have also given us the power to pollute and destroy the face of the earth.

ALL: **You make clear that each one of us has a part to play if our children and grandchildren are to inherit a good earth.**

ONE: You call us to responsibility.

ALL: **Creator, in this New Year we will carefully tend our small corner of the world and keep creation worthy of your glorious name. Amen.**

A Prayer of Compassion *(from Matthew 25:31–40)*

ONE: You call on us to care passionately for those in our church and for those in our community who are most at risk.
You call us to care for those who are hungry or thirsty.

ALL: **We will provide food and drink when both are hard to come by.**

ONE: You call us to acknowledge the stranger, and to welcome the refugee.

ALL: **We will welcome the newcomer warmly and give refuge to those who have been forced to flee.**

ONE: You call us to clothe those whose clothes are inadequate for their needs.

ALL: **We will give money for shoes and strong garments to those who ask.**

ONE: You call us to visit the prisoners and to support their families.

ALL: **We will speak of change rather than of punishment. We will advocate for treatment for the mentally sick and find work for those who have been released.**

ONE: In caring for these people who are at risk, we care for Jesus.

ALL: **"Whenever you did this for one of the least important of these sisters or brothers of mine, you did it for me."** *(time of silent reflection)*

Assurance of Action

ONE: You see the needs of those around you. Will you work with the insight of Jesus Christ to meet those needs?

ALL: **Our eyes are open to the plight of the hungry, the newcomer, to those without adequate clothing, and to prisoners. We will get started.**

ONE: You will work as a faith community and you will find your own way to help.

ALL: **God will bless all we do in the way and the name of Jesus. Amen.**

Offering Prayer

ONE: You blessed our giving in the year that is over, loving God. Our gifts brought help and comfort to the needy ones of this faith community, and, through the mission

fund, to suffering and downtrodden people throughout the world.

ALL: **We thank you for the opportunity to share our gifts
and we ask that our giving in the coming year will meet
the needs that are clearly set before us.**

ONE: The loving God who blessed you in days gone by will
keep you faithfully responsive to future challenges. You
are a church family of generous givers and in giving
you receive. Amen.

or

Offering Prayer

ONE: You will bless our gifts, loving God. Give joyfully.

ALL: **We will receive thankfully.**

ONE: Give carefully.

ALL: **We will receive generously.**

ONE: Give thoughtfully.

ALL: **We will receive gracefully.**

ONE: Give wholeheartedly.

ALL: **We will receive faithfully. Amen.**

 ### Pastoral Prayer Pattern

ONE: What does it mean to be God's people?

ALL: **It means to care compassionately.**

ONE: The hungry of this nation and those in *(name location)*
lift their hands, begging, imploring us to provide food.

ALL: **How will we respond?**

ONE: Those who need water cry out for the resource we take
for granted: water to drink, water with which to wash.

ALL: **How will we respond?**

ONE: Indigenous people on isolated reserves who lack basic
resources, and youngsters who lack a reason to live,
call out for help.

ALL: **How will we respond?**

ONE: What does it mean to be God's people?

ALL: **It means to care compassionately.**

ONE: What does it mean to be God's people?

ALL: **It means to care compassionately.**

ONE: The immigrant in an alien land, the refugee far from home, are coping with a different culture, different ways.

ALL: **How will we respond?**

ONE: The person suddenly taken ill faces a hospital routine far different from home, faces pain and treatment that is hard to endure.

ALL: **How will we respond?**

ONE: The person who has suffered sudden loss does not know where to turn, the long-grieving one needs someone to stay with them.

ALL: **How will we respond?**

ONE: What does it mean to be God's people?

ALL: **It means to care compassionately.**

Commissioning

ONE: You are a New Year's people. Live up to your high calling. Learn from the past.

ALL: **We will question vigorously, we will remember carefully, we will forgive bigheartedly.**

ONE: Act faithfully in the present.

ALL: **We will accept without discrimination, we will support consistently, we will meet suffering with compassion.**

ONE: Look to a Christ-following future.

ALL: **We will be open to new approaches, we will search thoroughly, we will be ready for opposition, we will meet conflict with love.**

ONE: God will accept you. God will strengthen you. God will bless you.

Go with God into the New Year. You have nothing to fear.

or

New Year Commissioning

ONE: Go into this New Year with confidence.

ALL: We go confidently, for God goes with us.

ONE: Know calm in the struggle,
      know patience when you feel vulnerable and
      frustrated,
      know the support of loved ones when hard times hit
      home,
      know the support of friends in the lonely moments,
      and know God's limitless love when you feel the limits
      of this time and space.

ALL: We go into this New Year in peace.

Epiphany Sunday

(Years A, B, C)

Isaiah 60:1–6
Psalm 72:1–7, 10–14
Ephesians 3:1–12
Matthew 2:1–12

The star-following visitors from the East find the Christ child

Call to Worship

ONE: People of the light, come and worship.

ALL: **We have the light of Christ to guide us.**

ONE: People of the light, strengthen each other.

ALL: **We have the light of Christ at the heart of our faith community.**

ONE: People of the light, listen to God's Word.

ALL: **We have the light of Christ to turn words to action.**

ONE: People of the light, know God's love for you and with you.

ALL: **We have the light of Christ in whom God's love is wonderfully present.**

ONE: People of the light, come and worship.

Opening Prayer

ONE: Rejoice with the Magi as you look for the Christ-child.

ALL: **Jesus is worth the search, worth the struggle to find.**

ONE: Rejoice with the Magi as you approach the Christ-child.

ALL: **Born to humble parents, yet the Christ-child's life is beyond price.**

ONE: Rejoice with the Magi as your present your gifts to the Christ-child.

ALL: **The world is still needing gifts inspired by God's chosen one.**

ONE: Rejoice with the Magi as you return home from Bethlehem.

ALL: **The light that shone from the stable still shines, and the light overcomes the darkness. Amen.**

A Prayer of Epiphany Questions

ONE: The Magi are willing to journey and to risk in order to find God's chosen one.
Herod is afraid of a rival.

ALL: **Do we risk going a new way or does our fear get the better of us?** *(time of silent reflecction)*

ONE: The Magi are ready to honour the wonder-full child. Herod is determined to destroy Jesus.

ALL: **Do we acknowledge the highest good, the right way, or do we look away?** *(time of silent reflecction)*

ONE: The Magi's gifts are given generously and symbolically. Herod lies about his intentions.

ALL: **Are we willing to offer with straightforward generosity, or do we have a hidden agenda?** *(time of silent reflecction)*

ONE: The Magi have no time for the self-serving, malicious ruler and his crew. Herod is the power person and insists he must be obeyed.

ALL: **Can we stand up to the power people or do we find excuses and give in.** *(time of silent reflecction)*

Assurance of Change

ONE: The Magi were wise and they were certain of their mission. They were not intimidated or fearful. They knew their journey was right and they reached their destination.

ALL: **God will go with us on our just and faithful journeys and give us the spiritual strength to persevere.**

ONE: God will deal with your timidity and lack of confidence.

ALL: **We will go forward unafraid. Amen.**

Offering Prayer

ONE: You give gifts of money, time, and talent for blessing.

ALL: **God gives us endurance on the journey, light in the dark places, a willingness to be humble and to stand with the humble.**

ONE: God goes with you.

ALL: **We will counter the powerful, expose the deceitful, and protect those who are at risk.**

ONE: Your gifts will be received and blessed.

ALL: **Amen.**

 ## Pastoral Prayer Pattern

ONE: The Magi followed the star with faithful determination.

ALL: **Living God, where will the star lead us?**

ONE: Determination: we pray for dedicated medical research personnel.
We think of those who are working to end one of the many cancers.
Determination: we pray for family members who continue to speak up for children and for elderly people who cannot speak up for themselves.
Determination: we pray for those who endure pain, and for doctors who persist in relieving pain without addiction-causing drugs.
Determination: we remember those in our close family or friendship circles who are fighting disease and sickness, and those in our faith community. *(time of silence)*
Determination: we pray for those who have lost loved ones, especially those who continue to experience the throbbing ache of bereavement. *(time of silence)*
The magi followed the star with faithful determination.

ALL: **Living God, where will the star lead us?**

ONE: The Magi followed the star with faithful determination.

ALL: **Living God, where will the star lead us?**

ONE: We are open to new forms of evangelization, fresh ways of being church.

We are ready to encourage children and young persons to ask their faith questions, and to listen to their insights and gospel songs.

We will encourage those with talents to use them within the church, and in the service of Christ in the neighbourhood.

We will provide training for those who teach and lead within the congregation, with the faithful determination of the Magi.

The Magi followed the star with faithful determination.

ALL: **Living God, where will the star lead us?**

Commissioning

ONE: Go from here with the amazement of the Magi.

ALL: **God's way can be found and followed.**

ONE: Go from here with the amazement of the Magi.

ALL: **God's promised one has been born to humble parents far from home.**

ONE: Go from here with the amazement of the Magi.

ALL: **The dark powers are no match for God's wise ones.**

ONE: Go from here with the amazement of the Magi.

ALL: **Dreams can become reality when we have insight and resolve.**

1st Sunday after the Epiphany

Baptism of Jesus

Isaiah 43:1–7
Psalm 29
Acts 8:14–17
Luke 3:15–17, 21–22

John foretells the significance of Jesus

Call to Worship
ONE: Come to the Jordan River.
ALL: **Listen to John, the fearless prophet.**
ONE: Come to the Jordan River.
ALL: **See the prophet who recognizes the significance of Jesus.**
ONE: Come to the Jordan River.
ALL: **Rejoice as Jesus and the people are baptized by John.**
ONE: Come to the Jordan River.
ALL: **The Holy Spirit is ready to bring change.**

Opening Prayer
ONE: Loving God, thank you for John, extraordinary prophet of his time.
ALL: **Give to each one of us prophetic power.**
ONE: Prophetic power:
ALL: **insight to see the best in those we meet.**
ONE: Prophetic power:
ALL: **courage to confront the arrogant and those who bully.**
ONE: Prophetic power:
ALL: **a willingness to bring together the suffering and downtrodden.**

ONE: Prophetic power:

ALL: the ability to speak up for the disillusioned, the challenged, and the infirm.

ONE: John will be your prophetic inspiration.

ALL: We will follow faithfully. Amen.

A Prayer of Choice

ONE: As Jesus is clearly identified as God's beloved, chosen by God, God has chosen us to be about God's work in our time and our situation. Like Jesus, we will discover our calling. God has called us; we will respond.

ALL: Has God called us to be still in prayer and in silent meditation, to listen carefully for God's voice? *(time of silent reflecction)*

ONE: God has called you and you will respond.

ALL: Has God called us to end conflicts and grudges within the family circle? *(time of silent reflecction)*

ONE: God has called you and you will respond.

ALL: Has God called us to work with others in this faith community, to help the needy of this neighbourhood? *(time of silent reflecction)*

ONE: God has called you and you will respond.

ALL: Has God called us to discover the effect of climate change on our part of this troubled planet? *(time of silent reflecction)*

ONE: God has called you and you will respond.

ALL: Has God called you to help those who have a low opinion of their own skills and abilities? *(time of silent reflecction)*

ONE: God has called you and you will respond.

A Prayer of Faithful Response to Calling

ONE: You are the people of God. You are called to go about God's work.

**ALL: We will listen carefully.
We will risk courageously.**

We will work together.
We will ignore the doubters.
We will support the struggling.
We will seek help from the wise ones.

ONE: You will find joy as you go about God's work.

ALL: **Thanks be to God. Amen.**

Offering Prayer

ONE: You bring to God the gifts of those who have been baptized.

ALL: **The gifts of friendship and support within the faith community.**

ONE: God welcomes your gift.

ALL: **The gifts of prayer and praise and study of the Word.**

ONE: God welcomes your gift.

ALL: **The gifts of money, time, and talent, for use here and where the mission fund is effective.**

ONE: God welcomes your gift.

ALL: **The gift of working alongside prisoners, children, those in care homes, and others who are striving to find their voice.**

ONE: God welcomes your gifts.
        In baptism you receive God's blessing,

ALL: **and God's blessing is received with these gifts. Amen.**

 ## Pastoral Prayer Pattern

ONE: We are followers of God's chosen one, Jesus.

ALL: **We will work in the way of Jesus Christ.**

ONE: We will link hands with those who are forced to work in dangerous places.
        We will support those who are persecuted for their stand against the powerful. *(current example)*
        We will protest against those who deny medical services to those who need them.
        We will speak out against the poisoning of lakes and oceans. We will hold water to be holy.

We are followers of God's chosen one, Jesus.

ALL: **We will work in the way of Jesus Christ.**

ONE: We are followers of God's chosen one, Jesus.

ALL: **We will work in the way of Jesus Christ.**

ONE: We will prepare for our discipleship in silence and in prayer, and will follow the example of saints ancient and modern.

We will respect the time available to work with our faith community members and will not pressure them to do more.

We will be on the lookout for the despised and rejected in our communities and we will support them.

We will laugh with our fellow disciples and enjoy eating with them.

We are followers of God's chosen one, Jesus.

ALL: **We will work in the way of Jesus Christ.**

Commissioning

ONE: You are God's chosen ones. Rejoice!

You have been chosen to listen to the wise ones.

ALL: **We have been chosen to be the prophets of today.**

ONE: You have been chosen to work with others in faith community.

ALL: **The water of baptism secures us and enlivens all we do together.**

ONE: You have been chosen to search for justice and to act with compassion.

ALL: **We will work as true followers of Jesus the Christ.**

ONE: You are God's chosen ones.

ALL: **We rejoice that we go from this church in the spirit of the saints.**

We go forward unafraid.

2nd Sunday after the Epiphany

Isaiah 62:1–5
Psalm 36:5–10
1 Corinthians 12:1–11
John 2:1–11

A wonderful sign at the wedding in Cana

Call to Worship

ONE: Come to worship.
ALL: **We come to celebrate in our worship.**
ONE: Come to celebrate.
ALL: **We come to celebrate with our friends.**
ONE: Come to celebrate with your friends.
ALL: **We come to hear God's Word for our faith community.**
ONE: Come to hear God's Word.
ALL: **We come to bring God's Word alive through our actions.**

Opening Prayer

ONE: A sign of the presence of Jesus:
ALL: **joy at a wedding in Galilee.**
ONE: A sign of the presence of Jesus:
ALL: **concern when what was essential was not there.**
ONE: A sign of the presence of Jesus:
ALL: **every person receives what they need.**
ONE: A sign of the presence of Jesus:
ALL: **the glory of Jesus becomes clear.**
ONE: A sign of the presence of Jesus:
ALL: **the way of Jesus is faithfully followed. Amen.**

A Prayer of Radical Change

ONE: A sign of Jesus:

ALL: **water into wine.**

ONE: A sign of Jesus:

ALL: **panic into calm.**

ONE: A sign of Jesus:

ALL: **joy where there was anxiety.**

ONE: A sign of Jesus:

ALL: **the best where it was ordinary.**

ONE: A sign of Jesus:

ALL: **healing where there was suffering.**

ONE: A sign of Jesus:

ALL: **compassion where there was indifference.**

ONE: A sign of Jesus:

ALL: **acceptance where there was rejection.**

ONE: A sign of Jesus:

ALL: **justice where power ruled supreme.**

ONE: A sign of Jesus:

ALL: **the cross when it should have been glory time.** *(time of silent reflection)*

ONE: A sign of Jesus:

ALL: **hope that death cannot defeat.**

Words of Assurance

ONE: You are the ones who see the signs of Jesus in our time.

ALL: **We are the ones who can bring radical change.**

ONE: Loving God,

ALL: **give us the courage that will conquer apathy and fear; give us the courage to say the words that are needed; give us the courage to act on what we see and experience; give us patient endurance when change comes slowly.**

ONE: You will be the signs of Jesus for your time.

ALL: **We will, thanks be to God. Amen.**

Offering Prayer

ONE: Celebrate as you bring your gifts to God.

ALL: **We celebrate that we have money, time, and talent to give.**

ONE: Celebrate as you bring your gifts to God.

ALL: **We celebrate that we can offer our gifts in a faith community.**

ONE: Celebrate as you bring your gifts to God.

ALL: **We celebrate the difference our gifts make to those in our church who are suffering and to those who know a numbing sense of loss.**

ONE: Celebrate as you bring your gifts to God.

ALL: **We celebrate as our gifts go to work in our local community and beyond this nation through the mission fund.**

ONE: Loving God,

ALL: **we celebrate the difference our gifts will make. Amen.**

🌍 Pastoral Prayer Pattern

ONE: A sign of the holy,

ALL: **Jesus brings joy where there was fear.**

ONE: Where there is repression,

ALL: **Jesus brings freedom.**

ONE: We pray for *(contemporary example)*.

ALL: **Where there is conflict, Jesus brings peace.**

ONE: We pray for *(contemporary example)*.

ALL: **Where there is disaster, Jesus brings renewal.**

ONE: We pray for *(contemporary example)*.

ALL: **Where there is self-serving, Jesus brings care for others.**

ONE: We pray for *(contemporary example)*.
A sign of the Holy,

ALL: **Jesus brings joy where there was fear.**

ONE: A sign of the holy,

ALL: **Jesus brings joy where there was fear.**

ONE: In our moments of panic and deep anxiety, Jesus
       brings peace;
       when illness gets us down, Jesus bring good friends we
       can talk to;
       when the bills and statements of debt are a burden,
       Jesus brings strength to face the situation;
       when dreams come to nothing, Jesus brings the willing-
       ness to glimpse a new vision.
       A sign of the holy,

ALL: **Jesus brings joy where there was fear.**

Commissioning

ONE: Go from this church in the spirit of Jesus Christ.

ALL: **We will be part of celebrations and enjoy them hugely.**
       We will be called on to bring change for good and will
       not hold back.
       We will use our talents to bring order from chaos.
       We will be a sign of all that is most generous and
       caring.
       We will wear the cross of Jesus humbly, and follow his
       way faithfully.

ONE: The spirit of Christ is yours. Rejoice and be glad!

3rd Sunday after the Epiphany

Nehemiah 8:1–3, 5–6, 8–10
Psalm 19
1 Corinthians 12:12–31a
Luke 4:14–21

Jesus begins his work

Call to Worship

ONE: Friends in the Spirit, come and worship.

ALL: **We give thanks as we offer praise and prayer.**

ONE: Friends in the Spirit, know the peace of God.

ALL: **In the quiet of this place, we approach the Holy One.**

ONE: Friends in the Spirit, listen for God's Word.

ALL: **God has a special word for us; we will listen.**

ONE: Friends in the Spirit, God has work for you to do.

ALL: **We will use our gifts and talents in God's service.**

Opening Prayer *(from Luke 4:14–21)*

ONE: Jesus brought the Good News to the people of his time.

ALL: **We are called to bring the Good News to people of our time.**

ONE: Jesus brought Good News to the poor.

ALL: **We are called to encourage the sharing of this world's goods.**

ONE: Jesus proclaimed freedom to those who were captive.

ALL: **We are called to set free those who are bound by tradition or addiction.**

ONE: Jesus gave sight to the blind.

ALL: **We are called to be the bringers of insight and fresh understanding.**

ONE: Jesus set free the oppressed.

ALL: **We are called to speak and act for people who face discrimination because of their age, race, or gender.**

ONE: Loving God,

ALL: **like Jesus, help us to be Good News bringers. Amen.**

A Prayer for the Body of Christ
(from 1 Corinthians 1:12–31)

ONE: Each one of us is needed in the body of Christ.

ALL: **The "eyes" are the ones who see the downhearted and help them. They advocate for the downtrodden.**

ONE: Each one of us is needed in the body of Christ.

ALL: **The "feet" are those who do the small but essential tasks: count the money, open the church, make the coffee.**

ONE: Each one of us is needed in the body of Christ.

ALL: **The "heads" take on leadership roles in the faith community: with youth, with children, serving on the board or council. They are willing to take responsibility.**

ONE: Each one of us is needed in the body of Christ.

ALL: **The "guts" are those who participate in worship, in Bible study groups, and who are ready to write for the release of political prisoners. Without them the Christian body would fail to function.**

ONE: Each one of us is needed in the body of Christ.

ALL: **The "hearts" are the pastoral caregivers and those who have a compassionate vision for the faith community.**

ONE: No member is better than another; all are essential. We are all able to contribute our varied talents, and we are each able to sustain the other.

ALL: **If one member suffers a personal setback, we feel that setback.**
If one member loses a loved one, we will stand beside the one who has suffered loss.

If one member suffers from ill health, we will encour-age and help that person. *(time of silent reflection)*

ONE: "You are all Christ's body, and each one of you is a part of it," writes Paul.

ALL: **Thanks be to God.**

Assurance of a Vital Faith Community

ONE: There is work for each person to do to build up the faith community.

ALL: **We will take stock of our talents and use them in the service of Jesus Christ.**
We will search out the newcomer and, in due time, ask them to serve.
We will be ready to help each other and to encourage the downhearted.
We will support the leaders and thank them carefully.
We will be aware of the needs of our neighbourhood and help meet those needs.
We will be aware of the needs of the wider church and will give to meet those needs.

ONE: And the mission of the church will be enlivened.
Amen.

Offering Prayer

ONE: We are your people, loving God.
Through us your Good News is made known.

ALL: **We tell the Good News to our friends and family members.**
We proclaim fresh vision and freedom to our neighbours.
We have words of hope for those who are suffering or poor.

ONE: Your gifts make change for the better possible.
God blesses your gifts; God blesses you.

ALL: **Thanks be to God. Amen.**

Pastoral Prayer Pattern

ONE: God's Spirit is with us,

ALL: **as we continue the ministry of Jesus.**

ONE: We will make sure that those who are most vulnerable are treated as well as anyone else.

We will make sure that those who are held back because of a challenge to their ability are heard and helped.

We will make sure that the sick who do not understand their diagnosis or treatment find out what is going on.

We will make sure that those who are oppressed find freedom.

We will make sure that the bereaved are supported in their time of loss.

God's Spirit is with us,

ALL: **as we continue the ministry of Jesus.**

ONE: God's Spirit is with us,

ALL: **as we continue the ministry of Jesus.**

ONE: We have a ministry with those oppressed because of their sexual orientation.

We have a ministry with those struggling to find their faith and to put their faith into action.

We have a ministry with Indigenous peoples.

We have a ministry with those who are newcomers to our nation.

We have a ministry with those most at risk in our neighbourhood.

We have a ministry with those most at risk in our faith community.

And all of these people will minister to *us*.

God's Spirit is with us,

ALL: **as we continue the ministry of Jesus.**

Commissioning

ONE: Go out as those committed to change in the Christian way.

At home, at work, at your social group, or on the street, make clear what you have heard in church.

ALL: **We will support and encourage the poor.**

We will open the eyes of those blinded by prejudice or upbringing.

We will show the way of freedom to those who are held bound.

We will lift the burden from the anxious and oppressed.

ONE: Know this for sure: "The time has come when God will save God's people."

4th Sunday after the Epiphany

Jeremiah 1:4–10
Psalm 71:1–6
1 Corinthians 13:1–13
Luke 4:21–30

Jesus is rejected by the people of his home town

Call to Worship

ONE: We come to worship the one eternal God.

ALL: **Source and origin of creation, God is with us today.**

ONE: We come to give thanks for all God's gracious gifts,

ALL: **found in family and relationship, sustaining us in tough times and in times of celebration.**

ONE: We come to listen to the truth in scripture,

ALL: **spoken clearly in the teaching of Jesus. We hear God's Word and we pay attention.**

ONE: We come to receive God's challenge,

ALL: **difficult and dangerous in the time of Jesus. God's challenge calls us to hard and faithful work today.**

Opening Prayer *(from Jeremiah 1:4–10)*

ONE: Loving God, you know us through and through; you want us to speak for you.

ALL: **We are surprised that you call us. We are surprised that you want us to do your good and compassionate work.**

ONE: We are not sure we have the maturity or the ability.

ALL: **We are afraid we will not measure up. We are not sure we have the endurance.**

ONE: But you give us the self-assurance we need, the authority to speak for you.

ALL: **We will speak out for the suffering refugee, and against the spoiling of planet Earth.**

ONE: We will speak with confidence; we will take courage from our leader Jesus;

ALL: **and we will bring honour to your holy name. Amen.**

A Prayer of Love *(from 1 Corinthians 13:1–3)*

ONE: Eternal God, your divine nature is love, total love, all-encompassing love, nothing but love.

ALL: **Loving God, we adore you.**

ONE: You may be the most silver-tongued speaker, moving crowds with your words,

ALL: **but without love it will get you nowhere.**

ONE: You may be the smartest person in your group, having the highest level of education,

ALL: **but without love it doesn't mean a thing.**

ONE: You may have the most generous nature, supporting charity after charity,

ALL: **but if love is not at the core of your giving, it simply doesn't count.**

ONE: You may sacrifice for the needs of others, giving up your cherished dreams,

ALL: **but if sacrifice doesn't stem from a loving nature it will fail.**

ONE: Love is patient and kind; it is not jealous or conceited or proud.
Love is not ill-mannered or selfish or irritable.

ALL: **Love does not keep a record of wrongs. Love is not happy with evil but is happy with the truth.**

ONE: Love never gives up and its faith, hope, and patience never fail.
Love is eternal. *(time of silent reflection)*
The loving way is the way we aspire to God.

ALL: **Love you will grant us, God, through the Spirit. Your Love is our love to receive.**

ONE: There are barriers to love in our personality; our

selfishness gets in the way; our own agenda rules; our pride sometimes gets the upper hand.

ALL: **But your love will conquer all obstacles and bring an end to our fear.**

ONE: "These three remain: faith, hope, and love. And the greatest of these is love."

ALL: **Amen.**

Offering Prayer

ONE: Jesus was rejected by the hometown crowd.

ALL: **We stand with the rejected ones and our gifts help.**

ONE: Our gifts help those of our faith community who feel alone.

ALL: **They speak of welcoming; they foster inclusion; they work to provide mutual cooperation and respect.**

ONE: Our gifts help those in our neighbourhood who have been ignored and forgotten.

ALL: **They speak of practical support; they foster action; they work with the very old, the youngest, and those at risk.**

ONE: Our gifts help those in the wider faith community who need a friend.

ALL: **They speak of global compassion; they remind us of our huge resources; they make it clear that suffering knows no borders.**

ONE: Bless these rejection-fighting gifts, loving God.

ALL: **Amen.**

 ### Pastoral Prayer Pattern *(from Luke 4:25)*

ONE: We will listen to the voices we trust.

ALL: **In these voices, we will hear God's voice:**

ONE: the voices that remind us of those who are without homes because of war.
We pray for those in *(contemporary situation)*.
We will hear God's voice in the voices that insist we pay attention to the sources of climate change.

We pray for *(contemporary situation)*.
We will hear God's voice in the voices that speak out
for the working poor, the voices that will not be
silenced because the powerful don't like what they say.
We pray for *(contemporary situation)*.
We will listen to the voices we trust.

ALL: **In these voices, we will hear God's voice.**

ONE: We will listen to the voices we trust.

ALL: **In these voices, we will hear God's voice:**

ONE: the voices that offer us calm in the midst of discord
and conflict,
the voices that encourage us to seek appropriate
medical care,
the voices that speak up for those who have memory
loss and dementia,
the voices that listen to our deepest fears,
the voices that comfort us in loss,
the voices that gently stay with us in bereavement.
We will listen to the voices we trust.

ALL: **In these voices, we will hear God's voice.**

Commissioning

ONE: Love generously,

ALL: **for God is love.**

ONE: Love patiently,

ALL: **for God is love**

ONE: Love justly,

ALL: **for God is love.**

ONE: Love with kindness,

ALL: **for God is love.**

ONE: Love in community,

ALL: **for God is love**

ONE: Love as you work,

ALL: **for God is love.**

ONE: Love as you celebrate,

ALL: **for God is love.**

ONE: Love in joy,

ALL: **for God is love.**

ONE: As you love, so you will be loved,

ALL: **for God is love.**

or

Commissioning

ONE: You go with us as we leave this church, living God.

ALL: **We realize we may face unpopularity.**
          We know friends may be lost, but we are ready for the
          criticism, and we will state clearly what is right.
          We may be challenged within our community.
          We may be challenged outside our community, but we
          are prepared for the long haul and we are unafraid.

ONE: Upheld by the Holy Spirit, and encouraged by the
        example of Jesus, you do not go alone.

5th Sunday after the Epiphany

Isaiah 6:1–8, (9–13)
Psalm 138
1 Corinthians 15:1–11
Luke 5:1–11

The call to be disciples

Call to Worship

ONE: Hear the words of Jesus and trust.

ALL: Trust in the God to whom we bring praise and prayer.

ONE: Hear the words of Jesus and trust.

ALL: Trust that his way will lead and inspire you.

ONE: Hear the words of Jesus and trust.

ALL: Trust that there is faithful work to do with your name on it.

ONE: Hear the words of Jesus and trust.

ALL: Trust that in the good times and the tough times, God goes with you.

Opening Prayer

ONE: We hear the call of Jesus to the disciples and we hear the call to each of us,

ALL: a call to think deeply about our future.

ONE: The call comes to each of us,

ALL: a call to consider our friendships and relationships.

ONE: The call comes to each of us,

ALL: a call to dream of God's purpose with us, and for us.

ONE: The call comes to each of us,

ALL: a call to share in faith community.

ONE: The call comes to each of us,

ALL: **a call to ask what we can do to advance the mission of Jesus Christ.**

ONE: The call comes to each of us,

ALL: **a call to find a cause in our local community and to support it wholeheartedly.**

ONE: Have you heard the call? How will you respond?

ALL: **Amen.**

A Prayer of Discipleship

ONE: Jesus calls us to follow.

ALL: **We will follow with our hearts as well as with our minds.**

ONE: Jesus calls us to listen to his teaching.

ALL: **We will read the scriptures and listen to those who teach in the spirit of Jesus Christ.**

ONE: Jesus calls us to note carefully the change that his presence may bring:

ALL: **compassion where there is indifference, hope where there is despair, friendship where there is loneliness.**

ONE: Jesus calls us to work in community.

ALL: **We will support each other and strive together for the common good.**

ONE: We remember Jesus, but we cannot forget the cross.

ALL: **Are we ready for the sacrifice and the rejection the cross so clearly symbolizes?** *(time of silent reflection)*

Words of Assurance

ONE: Loving God, when our discipleship is spasmodic, you give us commitment.

ALL: **When our discipleship is lukewarm, you give us determination.**

ONE: When our discipleship is solitary, you give us Christian friends.

ALL: **When our discipleship is self-centered, you point us to neighbourhood concerns.**

ONE: When our discipleship is close to home, you show us the needs of a suffering world.

ALL: **The disciples became a power for good in the ancient world.**
You remind us that we can be a power for good in our place and in our time. Amen.

Offering Prayer

ONE: The disciples of Jesus gave unsparingly to support his just and compassionate work. We are called to do the same.
Loving God,

ALL: **you call us to use the talents we have and those we may develop in the service of Jesus.**
You call us to share our resources and our time in the service of Jesus.
You call us to use our laughter and our sorrow in the service of Jesus.
You call us to use our knowledge and our willingness to learn in the service of Jesus.
You call us to use our cooperation and our communities in the service of Jesus.

ONE: Your words, your actions and your money will be effective as you use them together as faithful disciples.

ALL: **And your blessing, loving God, will be received. Amen.**

Pastoral Prayer Pattern

ONE: Who will God send to do God's work?

ALL: **We will go. Send us!**

ONE: There is no one else to do God's work.

ALL: **We will use our talents, we will search within our abilities, and we will give of our very best to serve God.**

ONE: We will serve those who cannot control their own destiny because of war.
We will serve those whose dreams and deepest wishes cannot become reality.

We will serve those who have been accidentally injured.
We will serve those who need fresh skills for the
workplace.
We will serve those, young or old, who lack the
learning aptitude they need.
Who will God send to do God's work?

ALL: **We will go. Send us!**

ONE: Who will God send to do God's work?

ALL: **We will go. Send us!**

ONE: We will serve those who cannot remember the names
of their children and grandchildren.
We will serve who do not think they are worthy of
being served.
We will serve those who have lost confidence in their
medical professionals.
We will serve the chronically sick and those who have
been taken by surprise by their illness.
We will serve those who love others so much they have
no time to care for themselves.
Who will God send to do God's work?

ALL: **We will go. Send us!**

Commissioning

ONE: Go from here as those called to do Christ's work:

ALL: **ready to listen carefully and to respond,**
ready to confront and not give in,
ready to search out the depressed and downtrodden,
ready to stand beside those who have suffered loss,
ready to support the faith community,
ready to counter fear with assurance,
ready to face the darkness with Christian light.

ONE: Ready to proclaim to the whole world that God's love,
as we know it in Jesus the Christ, will win through.

6th Sunday after the Epiphany

If this is the Sunday before Ash Wednesday, this Proper may be replaced by the readings for the last Sunday after Epiphany, Transfiguration Sunday.

Jeremiah 17:5–10
Psalm 1
Corinthians 15:12–20
Luke 6:17–26

Jesus teaches and heals.

Call to Worship

ONE: God invites us to worship.

ALL: **Joyfully we worship with this faith community.**

ONE: God invites us to listen to the words of Jesus.

ALL: **We are challenged to learn and respond.**

ONE: God invites us to heal and support.

ALL: **We will stay compassionately with those who are suffering.**

ONE: God invites us to be still and know the peace of God.

ALL: **Our worship will include times of patient waiting.** *(time of silent reflection)*

Opening Prayer

ONE: Jesus prays before he chooses 12 disciples. We are reminded of the key place of prayer in our religious practice.
Be still, and know the presence of the Spirit.

ALL: **In the silence, we will listen for the voice of God.** *(time of silent reflection)*

ONE: Be still and know the presence of the Spirit.

ALL: **In the silence, God will be with us as a faith community.** *(time of silent reflection)*

ONE: Be still and know the presence of God.

ALL: **In the silence, we will express our deepest concerns.** *(time of silent reflection)*

ONE: Be still and know the presence of God.

ALL: **In the silence, we will offer God our heartfelt thanks.** *(time of silent reflection)*

ONE: As we speak, as we listen, as we worship,

ALL: **God is with us. Amen.**

A Prayer of Trust *(from Jeremiah 17:7–8)*

ONE: We trust you, God.

ALL: **From generation to generation you have been there for us.**

ONE: We trust you, creator God.

ALL: **You have given us life and the good Earth to sustain us.**

ONE: We trust you, God who chose Jesus.

ALL: **We have his way to follow, his life's pattern to inspire us.**

ONE: We trust you, God who sustains.

ALL: **We are rooted in your Word, enlivened by the Spirit.**

ONE: We trust you, forgiving God.

ALL: **We have gone our own way and have ignored your values, but you enable us to radically change.**

ONE: We trust you, challenging God.

ALL: **You have shown us the downhearted and the troubled, and have called on us to respond.** *(time of silent reflection)*

Assurance that We Can Trust God

ONE: A tree planted beside the water sends out roots and knows life and strength as the roots find nourishment.

ALL: **So we will trust God to sustain us.**

ONE: As the leaves of the tree stay green when drought comes, so God will sustain us in the trials and struggles of life.

ALL: **Thanks be to God. Amen.**

Offering Prayer

ONE: We offer these gifts for blessing, loving God.
As those who are poor receive support and practical help,

ALL: **our gifts will be blessed.**

ONE: As those who are hungry, here and overseas, get the nourishment they need,

ALL: **our gifts will be blessed.**

ONE: As those who are sorrowing and lost know a loving presence,

ALL: **our gifts will be blessed.**

ONE: As those who are rejected and despised find acceptance,

ALL: **our gifts will be blessed.**

ONE: As those who are downhearted find joy,

ALL: **our gifts will be blessed.**

ONE: God will bless us as we put these gifts to work.

ALL: **We will be about God's holy tasks. Amen.**

 ## Pastoral Prayer Pattern

ONE: Tap into the flowing spring that is the Holy Spirit.

ALL: **We will be restored, renewed, refreshed.**

ONE: To those weary of peace-bringing, the spring restores patient endurance.
To those who are tired of being rejected by powerful leaders, the spring calls for outside-the-box approaches.
For those who despair that our planet can be saved for future generations, the spring rallies us to work for our children and grandchildren.

To those fed up with supporting and being supported, the spring encourages relaxation.
Tap into the flowing spring that is the Holy Spirit.

ONE: Tap into the flowing spring that is the Holy Spirit.

ALL: **We will be restored, renewed, refreshed.**

ONE: To those unsure of which direction to follow in life, the spring offers the opportunity to stop, consider options, and make a faithful choice.
To those who are waiting for appropriate medical treatment, the spring offers measured but not limitless patience.
To those afraid to go for a diagnosis of their condition, the spring offers action and courage.
To those ashamed of their continuing grief, the spring offers reassurance that grieving takes time, and the challenge to meet with others who have suffered loss.
Tap into the flowing spring that is the Holy Spirit.

ALL: **We will be restored, renewed, refreshed.**

Commissioning

ONE: We trust God.

ALL: **In the hard places of life and in life's celebrations, we trust God.**
In moments of despair and in moments of great joy, we trust God.
When loved ones support us and when they forget us, we trust God.
When we stand firmly for what is right and when we weakly compromise, we trust God.
When we join with others in the work of Jesus Christ and when we go it alone, we trust God.

ONE: Nothing can separate us from God or from God's love.

ALL: **Nothing in all creation. We trust God.**

7th Sunday after the Epiphany

If this is the Sunday before Ash Wednesday, this Proper may be replaced by the readings for the last Sunday after Epiphany, Transfiguration Sunday.

Genesis 45:3–11, 15

Psalm 37:1–11, 39–40

1 Corinthians 15:35–38, 42–50

Luke 6:27–38

Love your enemies

Call to Worship

ONE: Leave your anxieties behind.

ALL: This is a community of support.

ONE: Leave your grudges behind.

ALL: This is a community of fresh starts.

ONE: Leave your prejudice behind.

ALL: This is a community where all are valued.

ONE: Leave your ill will behind.

ALL: This is a community where love is central.

ONE: Leave your discouragement behind,

ALL: This is a community of eternal hope.

Opening Prayer

ONE: Loving God, you call us to go the extra mile,

ALL: to forgive when a loved one has hurt us.

ONE: You call us to go the extra mile,

ALL: to listen to the words spoken in anger.

ONE: You call us to go the extra mile,

ALL: to try a new way, to go in a fresh direction.

ONE: You call us to go the extra mile,

ALL: **to bear the pain when it goes on and on.**

ONE: You call us to go the extra mile,

ALL: **remembering that for Jesus, it led to a cross. Amen.**

A Prayer of the Golden Rule

ONE: Jesus said, "Do to others as you would have them do to you."

When a friend or family member has fallen on hard times and asks for support,

ALL: **"do to others as you would have them do to you."**

ONE: When a community member needs a boost, a strong word of encouragement,

ALL: **"do to others as you would have them do to you."**

ONE: When a refugee family without resources comes to your attention,

ALL: **"do to others as you would have them do to you."**

ONE: When there is a difficult task in your neighbourhood that you have the talent to carry out,

ALL: **"do to others as you would have them do to you."**

ONE: When climate change is taking its toll and leadership is needed locally to speak out and initiate recycling,

ALL: **"do to others as you would have them do to you."**

ONE: When a family in your community has suffered the loss of a cherished dream or the loss of a loved one,

ALL: **"do to others as you would have them do to you."** *(time of silent reflection)*

Assurance that Change is Possible

ONE: The Golden Rule calls us to walk in another's shoes, to feel as another feels, to respond to need as we would want another to respond to us or to our community. It isn't easy.

ALL: **We will remember the Golden Rule.**
We will remember its application worldwide.

We will take note of those in our family, in our church, and in our neighbourhood who live by the Golden Rule.

ONE: Give thanks for them and follow their example.

ALL: **Amen.**

Offering Prayer

ONE: Your local gifts will be a healing presence in this faith community.

ALL: **They will bring comfort to those who are sick and hope to the dying.**
They will counter the loneliness of those who cannot get out and support those who have suffered loss.

ONE: Your mission gifts will bring a better life to those far from here:

ALL: **training to those who have no job, new opportunities for women and children, and a safe haven for refugees.**

ONE: Your gifts will be a blessing to those who receive them and God will bless you the givers.

ALL: **Amen.**

Pastoral Prayer Pattern

ONE: Receive God's blessing,

ALL: **by taking the challenging path.**

ONE: We will offer prayers publicly and in small groups and wait to see what happens.
We will determine how we can serve our fellow disciples of Jesus Christ, and how we are willing to be served by them.
We will search out neighbourhood groups that need compassionate support, and support them.
We will encourage our fellow church members to use untested talents and offer them training.
Receive God's blessing,

ALL: **by taking the challenging path.**

ONE: Receive God's blessing,

ALL: by taking the challenging path.

ONE: Forgive the person with whom you have a long-standing grudge.
Forgive yourself for a wonderful opportunity not taken.
Follow the dream that will require sacrifice of resources and time.
Gently leave the friend who is bringing you grief.
Approach the person whom fear has kept at a distance.
Receive God's blessing,

ALL: by taking the challenging path.

Commissioning

ONE: Rejoice! You are Golden Rule people.

ALL: We will pray unceasingly.
We will forgive generously.
We will live adventurously.
We will abandon anxiety.
We will share gracefully.
We will meet suffering compassionately.
We will love beyond limits.

ONE: And God will be your constant companion along the way.

Last Sunday after the Epiphany

Transfiguration Sunday

Exodus 34:29–35
Psalm 99
2 Corinthians 3:12 – 4:2
Luke 9:28–36, (37–43)

Jesus is transfigured

Call to Worship

ONE: We come to this holy place; transformation is possible here,

ALL: **a place of awesome encounter. A place of holy insight.**

ONE: New relationships become possible here,

ALL: **a place of fresh encounters, a place to leave the past in the past.**

ONE: A new outlook will start here,

ALL: **a place of fresh vision, a place of surprise and recognition.**

ONE: This faith community is open for change,

ALL: **a place of healing and forgiving, a place of hope for the suffering.**

ONE: Come to this holy place in prayer; you will go away inspired and changed.

or

Call to Worship

ONE: Are you ready for a wonderful encounter?

ALL: **God's love touches us and holds us in this place.**

ONE: Are you ready for a wonderful encounter?

ALL: **This is the time to look beyond the limits of everyday needs and wants.**

ONE: Are you ready for a wonderful encounter?

ALL: **The divine is reflected in those around us.**

ONE: Are you ready for a wonderful encounter?

ALL: **God will equip us for the challenges of our troubled world.**

ONE: Are you ready?

ALL: **With God we have nothing to fear.**

Opening Prayer

ONE: We come into your presence with uncertainly, loving God.

ALL: **We are not sure what you will require of us.**

ONE: We come into your presence with awe, loving God.

ALL: **Your glory is way beyond our understanding, but your compassion is closer than our hands and feet.**

ONE: We come into your presence with a willingness to serve, loving God.

ALL: **You give us the strength to meet the needs of our neighbour and a corner of the suffering world.**

ONE: You come into our presence with joy, loving God.

ALL: **All of life, all that lies in the realm of eternity, is for you, and with you, and gives you praise and thanksgiving.**

ALL: Amen.

A Prayer of Transformation

ONE: Loving God, you call us to take the steep path up the mountain and to be ready to see people in a changed way,

ALL: **a glorious way.**

ONE: Friends whom we saw as practical "doers" are revealed as reflective and spiritual,

ALL: **a glorious way.**

ONE: The family members who we remembered for their good deeds are revealed as people of constant prayer,

ALL: **a glorious way.**

ONE: Community members who have taken leadership roles to support the disadvantaged and infirm have shown their underlying faith

ALL: **in a glorious way.**

ONE: Casual attenders of worship who have spoken out and written to help refugees and political prisoners make clear their Christian outlook

ALL: **in a glorious way.** *(time of silent reflection)*
Loving God, where we have failed to see the spiritual foundation on which so many wonderful and compassionate actions are based, forgive us.

Assurance of Peace and Christian Action

ONE: The glorious way is God's gift to us.

ALL: **We will see loved ones and strangers with wonderful clarity.**
We will acknowledge the foundation that they have in Christ.

ONE: You will discover how your own faith informs and inspires your compassion and Christian action.

ALL: **And we will know God's peace, the peace that keeps us strong and that sends us to work faithfully in the name of Jesus.**
Thanks be to God. Amen.

Offering Prayer

ONE: You take us to a holy place, O God.

ALL: **Your inspired presence lifts us up and gives us new life.**

ONE: You bring us down to earth, O God.

ALL: **Through your eyes we see what needs to be done and we find the strength to begin.**

ONE: Bless these gifts, O God,

ALL: **through which the ordinary shines with your holy presence. Amen.**

 Pastoral Prayer Pattern

ONE: An encounter with the holy leads to transformation.

ALL: **We are ready to transform and to be transformed.**

ONE: We will stand beside the lonely people of our community and bring them into a welcoming community.
We will open a dialogue with our Indigenous neighbours and with those of other faiths.
We will open a dialogue with our non-Indigenous neighbours, and with those of other faiths.
We will encourage those who have leadership skills and give them training.
We will prayerfully come before the awesome mystery and be ready to receive an encounter that leads to transformation.

ALL: **We are ready to transform and to be transformed.**

ONE: An encounter with the holy leads to transformation.
You are ready to transform and to be transformed.

ALL: **When we see the way ahead but are afraid to venture out, loving God, transform us.
When we cannot put into words what we believe loving God, transform us.
When we talk up our faith but are not willing to act on what we believe, living God, transform us.
When we claim to be followers of the Christ but are not sure what that means, living God, transform us.**

ONE: You are ready to transform and to be transformed.

ALL: **Amen.**

Commissioning

ONE: You will be transformed by your mountaintop experience.

ALL: **As the disciples were led to the place of revelation, so we will know glorious change.**

ONE: You will be transformed.

ALL: **As Jesus met with key leaders from his people's past, so the Christian and Hebrew scriptures will speak directly to us today.**

ONE: You will be transformed.

ALL: **As the disciples were confused by the momentous happenings, so we need time and space to make sense of our Christian faith.**

ONE: You will be transformed.

ALL: **As Jesus went down the mountain and immediately got on with his healing work, so we are called to Christian action in our time and place.**

ONE: You *will* be transformed and you *will* transform.

Lent 1

Deuteronomy 26:1–11
Psalm 91:1–2, 9–16
Romans 10:8b–13
Luke 4:1–13

Jesus is sorely tested

Call to Worship

ONE: Lent is a time of meditation.

ALL: **Enable us to take the quiet time that we need, loving God.**

ONE: Lent is a time of prayer.

ALL: **Enable us to listen intently for you, loving God.**

ONE: Lent is a time for living simply.

ALL: **We will reflect carefully on our resources, loving God,**

ONE: Lent is a time to have Jesus before us.

ALL: **We meet in the shadow of the cross, loving God.**

Opening Prayer of Reflection

ONE: Jesus begins his ministry and is tempted.

ALL: **We reflect on the sources of our own temptation.** *(time of silent reflection)*

ONE: Jesus begins his ministry and encounters the forces of darkness.

ALL: **We reflect on the dark forces that bedevil our world.** *(time of silent reflection)*

ONE: Jesus begins his ministry and is alone.

ALL: **We reflect on those we know who are lonely.** *(time of silent reflection)*

ONE: Jesus begins his ministry knowing that temptation will return.

ALL: **We reflect on the spiritual practice that will defend us this Lent.** *(time of silent reflection)*

ONE: "Lead us not into temptation,

ALL: **but deliver us from evil." Amen.**

A Prayer of Challenge from the Temptation of Jesus

ONE: We live in a world where there is huge abundance and terrible shortage, where the millionaire's home can be seen from the refugee camp.

ALL: **What can we do to foster sharing?**

ONE: We live in a world where the power brokers prosper, where the gap between rich and poor is growing.

ALL: **Through political action, can we narrow that gap?**

ONE: We live in a world where the focus is on getting and spending and the needs of children and those who struggle with mental illness are put aside.

ALL: **How can we best advocate for the downtrodden?**

ONE: We live in a world where sensational events grab the headlines, where TV and movie stars dominate the public eye.

ALL: **What can we do to move the spotlight to women who are at risk, and to gay and lesbian people who live in fear?** (time of silent reflection)

Assurance of Change

ONE: The values that Jesus taught were simple values.

ALL: **Compassion will counter suffering, peace will counter fear, those who have no voice, no sphere of influence, are precious in God's sight. Powerful, self-serving political leaders will not prevail.**

ONE: The teaching of Jesus was well understood and his reward was death on a cross. The need for compassion, the need for peace, and the need for justice are as pressing today as in the time of Jesus.

ALL: **As disciples of God's chosen one, we are called to respond. Amen.**

Offering Prayer

ONE: We trust God, and we offer God our gifts of money, time, and talent, so that this faith community can be about God's work.

ALL: **Where the hungry are fed, we are about God's work. Where the sick are visited, we are about God's work. Where the powerful are brought low, we are about God's work.**

Where the forces of selfishness are challenged, we are about God's work .

Where God's name is praised, prayer is offered, and the Word is heard, we are about God's work.

Where the way of Jesus is followed faithfully, we are about God's work.

ONE: And you will receive God's blessing.

ALL: **Amen.**

 ### Pastoral Prayer Pattern

ONE: Compassionate God, lead us not into temptation.

ALL: **but deliver us from evil.**

ONE: The voice of the tempter says, "Helping the world's hungry is not your job; put your own nation first."

The voice of the tempter says, "The powerful are the ones who count."

The voice of the tempter says, "Spectacular events and spectacular people are the important ones, the ones that make headline news."

The voice of the tempter says, "I can give you all your heart desires; simply trust me."

We say, compassionate God, lead us not into temptation:

ALL: **but deliver us from evil.**

ONE: Compassionate God, lead us not into temptation,

ALL: **but deliver us from evil.**

ONE: The voice of the tempter says, "Leave Indigenous people to sort out their own problems."
The voice of the tempter says, "Why waste your time by sending letters of concern to your elected representative? They haven't time to read letters from people like you."
The voice of the tempter says, "The needs of those who are infirm or mentally challenged are not your responsibility."
The voice of the tempter says, "The pain will probably go away; don't bother to have it checked out."
The voice of the tempter says, "Quit talking about your loss; you should have gotten over it by now."
We say, compassionate God, lead us not into temptation:

ALL: **but deliver us from evil.**

Commissioning

ONE: Resist temptation; give Christ the glory.

ALL: **Nourish your soul as well as your body.**

ONE: Resist temptation; give Christ the glory.

ALL: **Realize that much power brings much responsibility.**

ONE: Resist temptation; give Christ the glory.

ALL: **Shun the spectacular;; stand beside the defeated and defenseless.**

ONE: Resist temptation; give Christ the glory.

ALL: **Christ's way leads to true community.**

ONE: Resist temptation, and know the peace of Christ.

Lent 2

Genesis 15:1–12, 17–18
Psalm 27
Philippians 3:17– 4:1
Luke 13:31–35
        or Luke 9:28–36

Jesus' courageous love of Jerusalem

Call to Worship

ONE: God of our Lenten days,

ALL: we worship you with deep, deep humility.

ONE: God of our Lenten days,

ALL: we worship you searching for peace.

ONE: God of our Lenten days,

ALL: we worship you in faith community.

ONE: God of our Lenten days,

ALL: we worship you looking to Jesus and to his Lenten journey.

Opening Prayer

ONE: If you trust God, you have nothing to fear.

ALL: We will experience hostility.

ONE: God will stay with you.

ALL: We will know loneliness.

ONE: God will stay with you.

ALL: We will have doubts.

ONE: God will stay with you.

ALL: We will face difficult decisions.

ONE: God will stay with you.

ALL: Our friends will leave us.

ONE: God will stay with you.

ALL: We trust God; we have nothing to fear. Amen.

Remembering the Journey of Jesus to Jerusalem: a Reflective Prayer

ONE: Loving God, take these experiences of Jesus on his journey to Jerusalem and show us the way we should go.

ALL: **Amen.**

ONE: Jesus has a wonderful and fulfilling ministry, a good life away from the capital city, but he knows his call is to go to Jerusalem,

ALL: **the call to fulfill what God is calling Jesus to do.** *(time of silent reflection)*

ONE: Jesus gathers a group of friends and disciples around him. They are teaching and caring, but Jesus senses that they will fail him when the hard times come.

ALL: **These people do not have the endurance needed when trouble confronts them.** *(time of silent reflection)*

ONE: The religious leaders and the governing power groups are threatened by one who is morally above reproach; they want him out of their way.

ALL: **The power of Jesus is the power of compassion, the power of love.** *(time of silent reflection)*

ONE: Despite many concerns, many regrets, many "if-onlys," Jesus sets out on his journey to the holy city, a journey that will end with him alone and on a cross.

ALL: **We know that God did not abandon Jesus, God's chosen one, though it felt that way to Jesus.** *(time of silence)*

Words of Assurance

ONE: Our fears, our apathy, our lack of courage matter to you, loving God, as do our determination, our faithfulness, and our patient persistence.

ALL: **As we go on our own journey to Jerusalem this Lent, go with us and guide us. Loving God, may we know that our destination is your destination for us. Amen.**

Offering Prayer

ONE: Loving God, we offer you our gifts for the journey of our faith community:

ALL: **gifts of money, for ministries of music, pastoral care, and reflection on your Word;**
gifts of time, to build up this community of faith and to support those suffering and bereaved within the fellowship;
gifts of talent, to provide leadership and assistance to those in this neighbourhood who are unemployed, struggling, and without adequate housing;
gifts of compassion for those far from here, refugees, at-risk families, oppressed women, and those without hope, for whom the mission fund is essential.

ONE: You have given freely and generously in the use of these gifts. You will be blessed. Amen.

 Pastoral Prayer Pattern

ONE: Jesus would not be deflected; he went to Jerusalem.

ALL: **Give us the willpower, living God, to go forward unafraid.**

ONE: We hear the words of those who stand with immigrants and refugees, and will not keep quiet.
We hear the warnings of those who are desperately worried about the emissions of gasses into the atmosphere, who clamour to be heard.
We see the efforts of people who will not be satisfied until no girl or boy goes to work instead of to school, people who speak out for these youngsters.
We are reassured by the reports of those who work with prisoners, who remind us that with patience and education, they are less likely to reoffend.
We are determined to be agents of change.
Jesus would not be deflected; he went to Jerusalem.

ALL: **Give us the willpower, living God, to go forward unafraid.**

ONE: Jesus would not be deflected; he went to Jerusalem.

ALL: **Give us the willpower, living God, to go forward unafraid.**

ONE: When we are reluctant to take time with the troubled and downhearted, give us the willpower, loving God.

When we hold back from saying the word that affirms, the word that encourages self-confidence, give us the willpower, loving God.

When we are aware of newcomers but fail to welcome them, give us the willpower, loving God.

When we are aware of the task to which we are called but fail to get on with it, give us the willpower, loving God.

Jesus would not be deflected; he went to Jerusalem.

ALL: **Give us the willpower, living God, to go forward unafraid.**

Commissioning

ONE: Take with you what you need for your Lenten journey: determination to walk the hard road that Jesus walked, joy that you have friends from this church with you, peace in prayer and meditation,

resources in the Bible and on the Internet to guide and challenge you,

memories of the good people who have been on the journey before you.

ALL: **We have what we need for our Lenten journey, and we rejoice that God goes with us.**

ONE: God's love surrounds you and will never let you go.

Lent 3

Isaiah 55:1–9
Psalm 63:1–8
1 Corinthians 10:1–13
Luke 13:1–9

If God's vision is ignored, trouble will follow

Call to Worship *(from Psalm 63)*

ONE: That deepest part of us, that most authentic part of us, that holy part of us, longs for you, living God.

ALL: **Sometimes it finds you here among Christ's people.
Sometimes it finds you as we look up at the starry sky on a clear night.
Sometimes it finds you in the murmuring of a newborn baby.
Sometimes it finds you in a celebration among family and friends.
Sometimes it finds you when we feel utterly alone.**

ONE: And when that deepest part of us has been touched and held, we are aware of the constant love of God, which is, "better than life itself."

ALL: **Come to us in these moments of worship, God of love, for we are only and always yours.**

Opening Prayer/Prayer of Approach
(from Isaiah 55)

ONE: God says, "Come everyone who is thirsty; here is water! "Come buy wine and milk; it will cost you nothing!"

ALL: **God is waiting for us; God will provide.**

ONE: God says, "Come to me my people, and you will have life!
"I will make a lasting covenant with you and bless you."

ALL: **God is offering us an enduring relationship, God is calling us to commitment.**

ONE: The psalmist says, "Turn to God and pray to him; those who need to change their lifestyle, now is the time."

ALL: **God is ready to forgive.**

ONE: God says, "My word is like the snow and the rain; they make the crops grow, seed for planting, and food to eat."

ALL: **God gives us the Word that feeds us body, mind, and spirit.**

ONE: "Cypress trees will grow where there are briers, and myrtle trees will come up in the place of thorns."

ALL: **The graciousness of God will last forever. Amen.**

A Prayer of Renewal

ONE: Lent – time for a fresh start:

ALL: **an opportunity to consider new ventures at home, the chance to widen the friendship circle.** *(time of silent reflection)*

ONE: Lent – time for a fresh start:

ALL: **an opportunity to put grudges in the past, a chance to forgive generously.** *(time of silent reflection)*

ONE: Lent – time for a fresh start:

ALL: **an opportunity to offer thanks to God, a chance to serve in the faith community.** *(time of silent reflection)*

ONE: Lent – time for a fresh start:

ALL: **an opportunity to work with the voiceless, a chance to learn from the challenged.** *(time of silent reflection)*

ONE: Lent – time for a fresh start:

ALL: **an opportunity to explore spiritual ways, a chance to encounter other faith groups and writings.** *(time of silent reflection)*

Assurance of Renewal *(prayed slowly)*

ONE: Loving God,

ALL: **we know we need to confess all that brings us down; we know we need forgiveness.** *(time of silent reflection)*

ONE: Loving God,

ALL: **we know we have fresh ways to go, fresh opportunities to take, fresh learnings to make our own.** *(time of silent reflection)*

ONE: Loving God, as we commit ourselves to renewal of body, mind, and spirit, we know that you are our willing and loving partner.

ALL: **Thank you. Amen.**

Offering Prayer

ONE: Loving God, we believe that these gifts present opportunities to build each other up and to strengthen and encourage those who feel discouraged.
We present them hopefully.
These gifts will go to work within the faith community:
(see examples below, but offer your own examples)

ALL: **training teachers and leaders of youth,**
befriending older adults,
visiting those who cannot come to church,
supporting those who lead worship,
being with the dying and bereaved,
celebrating with those who get married.

ONE: These gifts will go to work within the wider church:
(give examples from the work of your mission fund)
These gifts will go to work in this neighbourhood: *(give examples from your town or city)*

ALL: **supporting the food bank,**
providing space for Alcoholics Anonymous,
running a thrift store.

ONE: As these gifts go to work, your name is honoured, loving God, and the way of Jesus is followed.

ALL: **Amen.**

Pastoral Prayer Pattern *(from Isaiah 55:1–2)*

ONE: God says, listen now to me, come to me,

ALL: **and you will have life.**

ONE: God's Word has within it the words of truth.
We give thanks for good translators and commentators
who make the Word a powerful influence today.
God's Word brings the faith community together.
We give thanks that it also sends them out to serve in
the way of Christ.
God's Word is there for church family members going
through hard time.
We give thanks there is also encouragement for joy and
celebration.
God's Word is read Sunday by Sunday in the sanctuary.
We give thanks that it is here for individual Christians,
a source of hope and strength.
God says, listen now to me, come to me,
and you will have life.

ONE: God says, listen now to me, come to me,

ALL: **and you will have life.**

ONE: God says, Come, everyone who is thirsty, here is water.
God is present to the suffering in those who provide
good medical care and care for the spirit: doctors,
nurses and chaplains are God's helpers.
God is present to those suffering through mental
illness: those who are depressed, troubled, or trauma-
tized. Specialists and mental health nurses are God's
helpers.
God is present to the dying and the bereaved in
presence, in prayer, and in listening. Ministers and
grief therapists are God's helpers.
God says, listen now to me, come to me,

ALL: **and you will have life.**

Commissioning

ONE: Let us go from here with the commitment of Jesus:

ALL: **in place of self-serving, care for others;**
in place of half-truths, honesty;
in place of power, compassion;
in place of evasion, facts faced;
in place of upheaval, peace;
in place of loss, feelings expressed;
in place of the same old routine, celebration.
We go together; we will serve joyfully.

Lent 4

Joshua 5:9–12
Psalm 32
2 Corinthians 5:16–21
Luke 15:1–3, 11b–32

The parable of the lost son

Call to Worship

ONE: With you, O God,

ALL: **the lost will be found.**

ONE: With you, O God,

ALL: **the disheartened will know joy.**

ONE: With you, O God,

ALL: **the wanderers will come back home.**

ONE: With you, O God,

ALL: **the downtrodden will know celebration.**

ONE: With you, O God,

ALL: **the disillusioned will get their confidence back.**

Opening Prayer *(from 2 Corinthians 5:19)*

ONE: You are our friend, loving God;

ALL: **in despair, we can come to you.**

ONE: You are our constant friend, loving God;

ALL: **in the tough times you are there for us.**

ONE: You are our faithful friend, loving God;

ALL: **when others turn away, you listen to us.**

ONE: You are our reliable friend, loving God,

ALL: **When we have gone our own way, you welcome us back. Amen.**

The Nature of God's Love

ONE: This is the glory of your love, O God;

ALL: **it is trusting; it lets us go off on our own.**

ONE: This is the wonder of your love, O God;

ALL: we make mistakes, but it does not give up on us.

ONE: This is the amazing love that is yours, O God;

ALL: it neither judges nor condemns us.

ONE: This is the astonishing love that is yours, O God,

ALL: when we see the light, it calls us to celebrate.

ONE: This is the community of love we know, O God;

ALL: we find it as people of faith sharing together.

ONE: This is the personal love that is yours, O God;

ALL: it comes clear in the life of Jesus Christ. *(time of silent reflection)*

Assurance of God's Love for Us

ONE: The deepest waters cannot cover God's love.
The driest summer cannot shrivel up God's love.

**ALL: The harshest conflict cannot destroy God's love.
The most brutal dictator cannot crush God's love.**

ONE: Cancer in its worst form cannot overcome God's love, neither can personal disaster end God's love.

ALL: A far-too-early death cannot kill God's love; neither can bereavement, which seems to be never-ending.

ONE: God's love is personal, but also for the community of faith.
God's love is for us now and does not end when life ends.
God's love is beyond understanding, but it is eternal.

ALL: Thanks be to God. Amen.

Offering Prayer

ONE: God, whom we trust, bless this offering.

ALL: You have come to us in the struggle, and have been the way of peace.

ONE: You have come when we felt at our weakest and have been a source of strength.

ALL: You have come when we felt on our own, and offered us friendship.

ONE: You have come when we felt rejected and have offered
        us love.

ALL: **God in whom we trust, may people in this faith com-
        munity and those in need far from here be blessed by
        our gifts. Amen.**

 Pastoral Prayer Pattern

ONE: The love of a parent for their child –

ALL: **unconditional, enduring, forgiving love – is beyond
        price.**

ONE: For those parents whose children are at risk due to
        warfare we pray, remembering the children in *(name
        current conflict)*, we pray.

        For those children who are at risk in their homes, and
        for young women at risk in big cities *(name current
        situation)*, we pray.

        For parents who will not forgive, and for children who
        will not accept forgiveness, we pray. *(time of silence)*

        For ministers and counsellors who bring parents and
        children together, we pray. *(time of silence)*

        The love of a parent for their child –

ALL: **unconditional, enduring, forgiving love – is beyond
        price.**

ONE: How can we support and help parents and their
        children?

ONE: The love of a parent for their child –

ALL: **unconditional, enduring, forgiving love – is beyond
        price.**

ONE: We pray for parents of children who are challenged
        physically or mentally.

        We pray for men and women who wish they could
        become parents but who are not able to conceive or
        adopt.

We pray for children who are addicted to opioids or alcohol, and for their distraught parents.
The love of a parent for their child –

ALL: **unconditional, enduring, forgiving love – is beyond price.**

ONE: How can we support and help parents and their children?

Commissioning

ONE: We take God's love with us as we leave this church. Love will overcome our selfishness,

ALL: **and reach out to help others.**

ONE: Love will not dwell on past wrongs,

ALL: **but will rejoice in a new path taken.**

ONE: Love will not criticize easily,

ALL: **but will forgive generously.**

ONE: Love will not let go without a struggle,

ALL: **but will welcome back joyfully.**

ONE: In Jesus, love is to be found absolutely.

ALL: **For Jesus, we thank God unceasingly.**

Lent 5

Isaiah 43:16–21
Psalm 126
Philippians 3:4b–14
John 12:1–8

Mary anoints Jesus with expensive ointment

Call to Worship

ONE: God is generous beyond understanding.

ALL: **Praise God!**

ONE: God is the source of compassion.

ALL: **Praise God!**

ONE: God embraces the vulnerable.

ALL: **Praise God!**

ONE: God gives strength to the weakest.

ALL: **Praise God!**

ONE: God calms the troubled.

ALL: **Praise God!**
In our faith community,
in our closest family relationships,
in our true friendships,
in our venturing out,

ONE: God is there.

ALL: **Praise God!**

Opening Prayer of Thanksgiving

ONE: Let us pray.

ALL: **We have the gift of life.**
We have the gift of family.
We have the gift of good friends.
We have the gift of the saints.
Thanksgiving is ours, loving God.
We have the gift of church/faith community.

We have the gift of the Hebrew and Christian
scriptures.
We have the gift of discipleship.
We have the gift of mission.
Thanksgiving is ours, loving God.
As we give thanks we will sing.
As we give thanks we will care.
As we give thanks we will support each other.
As we give thanks we will be quiet.
As we give thanks we will stand with the downtrodden
and remember your goodness to us and to our church.
(time of silent reflection)

ONE: In all the changing scenes of life we are yours, loving
       God,
ALL: **Amen.**

A Prayer of Generous Giving

ONE: You call us to give generously, loving God:
ALL: **to give generously to family, and to those within our
       circle of loved ones.** *(time of silent reflection)*
ONE: You call us to share joyfully, loving God:
ALL: **to give from our resources, large or small, to those
       who need our help.** *(time of silent reflection)*
ONE: You call us to act compassionately, loving God:
ALL: **to care for those who are discouraged, or sick, or have
       suffered loss.** *(time of silent reflection)*
ONE: You call us to work faithfully, loving God:
ALL: **to remember the example of Jesus and to commit to
       the just and merciful way, even when it costs us
       significantly.** *(time of silent reflection)*

An Assurance of Generous Giving

ONE: Are you ready to be there for your loved ones, and to
       share with those who find money and kindness hard to
       come by?
ALL: **We are ready; we will share.**

ONE: Are you ready to act compassionately? Are you ready to work for justice among those who are fearful and despised?

ALL: **We are ready; we follow Christ, champion of the vulnerable.**

ONE: God's peace will be your peace. Amen.

Offering Prayer

ONE: Mary honoured the act of giving when she poured ointment on the head of Jesus.
Our giving is a holy action.

ALL: **Giving signifies our Christian commitment.**
Giving symbolizes our compassion.
Giving is at the heart of our community life.
Our giving goes beyond our imagining.
These gifts, and our act of giving, are blessed by God.
Amen.

❤️ Pastoral Prayer Pattern

ONE: You call us to serve,

ALL: **to serve with generosity.**

ONE: Loving God, you call us to be with our friends and family in their testing times, and to accept help when we need it ourselves.
You call us to support the poor and the challenged of our local community, and to receive help graciously when we need it.
You call us to remember those of our faith community who are sick and who are going through tough times, and to stick with them as they support us in turn. *(time of silent reflection)*
You call us to give to those who are bereaved, and to stay with them in the down and helpless days.
You call us to serve,

ALL: **to serve with generosity.**

ONE: You call us to serve,

ALL: **to serve with generosity.**

ONE: Loving God, we will give money generously to help people beyond our faith community, where the need is clear: people sleeping on the street in our neighbourhood, people displaced from their homes overseas, and those receiving help from our mission fund.

We will give time and our skills generously to those we count as friends, and to struggling family members.

We will give time and talent and money to our faith community, remembering especially those who can no longer come to church.

And you call us to give generously to meet our own needs of time: to enjoy art and drama and good music, to be with our young family members, to read, and surf the net, and relax, and to simply smell the roses.

You call us to serve,

ALL: **to serve with generosity.**

Commissioning

ONE: Don't dwell on the past; don't get hung up on what has happened.

Look expectantly, look confidently, to what is now possible.

ALL: **In Christ, those without hope will find hope.**

In Christ, those in wheelchairs will get everywhere.

In Christ, women and children will get the respect they deserve.

In Christ, the refugee will find a home,

In Christ, the infirm elderly person will find support.

In Christ, the mentally ill will know compassion.

Is this wishful thinking?

ONE: In the spirit of Christ, all is possible.

Lent 6

Palm/Passion Sunday

Liturgy of the Palms
Luke 19:28–40
Psalm 118:1–2, 19–29

Jesus is welcomed as he comes to Jerusalem

Liturgy of the Passion
Isaiah 50:4–9a
Psalm 31:9–16
Philippians 2:5–11
Luke 22:14–23:56
     or Luke 23:1–49

The last supper, arrest, trial, and crucifixion

Call to Worship (Palm Sunday)
ONE: Jesus is coming with the disciples to Jerusalem.
ALL: **God's promised one is on the way.**
ONE: Sing songs of joyful praise.
ALL: **It's celebration time!**
ONE: Give thanks to God for all Jesus has done.
ALL: **We will tell our friends; we will tell the strangers we meet.**
ONE: Some of the powerful ones are telling you to keep quiet.
ALL: **Jesus says, "If you keep quiet, the stones themselves will start to shout."** *(The congregation raise their palms and shake them shouting, "Praise God, alleluia! Welcome Jesus.")*

Opening Prayer *(Palm Sunday)*

ONE: This is a time of joy; this is a time of enthusiasm.

ALL: **We welcome Jesus from the bottom of our hearts.**

ONE: This is a time of joining with our friends; this is a time of faithful community.

ALL: **We are one as we welcome Jesus.**

ONE: This is a time of remembering; this is the time of celebration.

ALL: **In bread broken and as we take the cup, we are one in Christ.**

ONE: This is a time of recognition; this is a time for blessing.

ALL: **We give thanks for all Jesus has accomplished.**

ONE: This is a time for caution; this is a time for sorrow,

ALL: **Jesus will be tried and sentenced; the cross lies just ahead. Amen.**

A Prayer of Joy for Palm Sunday

ONE: Jesus is with us as we find relaxation in good movies, and in people who make us laugh.

ALL: **Jesus is with us in joy and laughter.**

ONE: Jesus is with us as we remember good times and retell funny family stories.

ALL: **Jesus is with us in joy and sharing.**

ONE: Jesus is with us as we meet as a faith community to eat and drink and sing well-loved songs.

ALL: **Jesus is with us in a joyful church.**

ONE: Jesus is with us as we take on power people and work with those who are downtrodden and distressed.

ALL: **Jesus is with us in joyful engagement.**

ONE: Jesus is with us as we joyfully gather around the communion table.

ALL: **Jesus is with us as we recall the last supper, as we recall those who once met there for Holy Communion; and Jesus is with us as we are spiritually equipped to go out as his joyful disciples.** *(time of silent reflection)*

Assurance of Joy

ONE: We remember the Jesus of laughter and good friends.
We remember Jesus, who welcomed people rejected by
the "respectable" people. Jesus was a happy person and
wished that all should feel welcomed and be happy.

ALL: **Loving God, take from us the critical spirit. Enable us
to bring friendship to those who feel alone, and joy to
those who have been or are being treated harshly by
life.**
**Bless us with the loving spirit that warms the hearts of
those we meet. Amen.**

Offering Prayer *(Palm Sunday)*

ONE: Such an outpouring of support for Jesus as he came
into the city; such love, such fervour, such trust for this
person!

ALL: **No one held back their enthusiasm, commitment was
wholehearted.**
**Loving God, we give a wholehearted offering this
morning, for we believe those who work in the way and
in the spirit of Jesus deserve nothing less. Amen.**

 ### Pastoral Prayer Pattern *(Palm Sunday)*

ONE: God's blessing is with Jesus and the disciples as they
enter Jerusalem,

ALL: **Jesus receives a royal welcome, but the joy is soon
gone.**

ONE: We pray for good rulers and just politicians, and for
those struggling for peace. *(contemporary situation)*
We pray for those whose human rights have been
trampled on, and for those who are imprisoned and
tortured for speaking out for the persecuted.
(contemporary situation)
We pray for those who peacefully protest, for those
who put a just cause above personal safety.
(contemporary situation)

We pray for those who tear down physical and political barriers between nations and individuals. *(name contemporary situation)*

In the courageous name of Jesus,

ALL: **we pray for those who speak and work for justice.**

ONE: God's blessing is with Jesus and the disciples as they enter Jerusalem.

ALL: **Jesus receives a royal welcome, but the joy is soon gone.**

ONE: We pray for those church leaders who advocate for the persecuted and despairing *(contemporary situation)*.

We pray for those in our congregation who care for and give to those who are infirm or physically and mentally challenged.

Those of us who work among the poor, the challenged and the struggling, give thanks for them.

We pray and we will work for a vision that includes the neighbourhood in our faith community vision.

We pray for a faith that keeps and promotes political action as an integral part of the "Christian" way of acting.

In the courageous name of Jesus,

ALL: **we pray for those who speak and work for justice.**

Commissioning *(Palm Sunday)*

ONE: May joy be yours as you leave this church.

ALL: **We have welcomed Jesus with enthusiasm.**

ONE: May thanksgiving be yours as you leave this church.

ALL: **Our commitment to Jesus has put our lives in perspective.**

ONE: May friendship be yours as you leave this church.

ALL: **We have been nurtured in this community of Jesus.**

ONE: May peace be yours as you leave this church –

ALL: **God's peace, there for us in the cruelest times of life.**

***

Call to Worship *(Passion Sunday)*

ONE: Jesus has been brought before Pilate, given a mock trial, and sentenced to death.

ALL: **Jesus is mocked; Jesus is crucified.**

ONE: Powerful leaders jeer at him; soldiers make fun of him.

ALL: **Jesus says, "Forgive them. They don't know what they are doing."**

ONE: And his last words are, "Into God's hands, I commit my spirit."

ALL: **We hear the words of the army officer in charge. He praises God and said "Certainly this man was innocent."**

ONE: There is terrible sorrow among those in the crowd, and the women disciples stay behind to be with Jesus.

ALL: **Even today, the sorrow touches our hearts.**

Opening Prayer *(Passion Sunday)*

ONE: The light of the world will be put out.

ALL: **We give thanks for the enlightening presence of Jesus.**

ONE: The friend of the friendless will be gone.

ALL: **We give thanks for Jesus, who was strength to the weak, and who stood with the lonely.**

ONE: The person of peace will be silenced.

ALL: **We give thanks for Jesus who confronted the evil-doers and who calmed the fearful.**

ONE: The person of compassion will be stilled.

ALL: **We give thanks for Jesus whose healing presence affects us still. Amen.**

A Prayer of the Cross

ONE: Jesus on the cross, utterly powerless,

ALL: **reminds us of our own situations of powerlessness, and of the powerless ones who we can help.**

ONE: Jesus on the cross, mocked by soldiers and leaders,

ALL: reminds us of the times when we are at the mercy of others, and of when other people are at our mercy.

ONE: Jesus on the cross, talking with an insightful criminal,

ALL: reminds us of those who stand with us in the toughest of times, reminds us of friends, and of those we didn't know were friends.

ONE: Jesus on the cross, watched at great risk by women followers,

ALL: reminds of how much loyalty and endurance count when hard times come to stay. *(time of silent reflection)*

Prayer of Assurance

ONE: We have our own crosses to bear.

ALL: **God will remind us of those who are able to support us.**
God will be a source of patient endurance.
God will give us the courage to face our challenges.
We will discover the way they may be overcome. Amen.

Offering Prayer *(Passion Sunday)*

ONE: At the crucifixion of Jesus, the leaders of the people offered smart remarks.
The soldiers offered jokes and mocked him. One of the criminals offered insults.

ALL: **Because Jesus would not conform to the traditional culture,**
because Jesus would not live and work in obscurity,
because Jesus stood with the poor and persecuted,
because Jesus was seen as the Messiah,
his life was ended by a cross death.
He could not have offered more.

ONE: As we offer our gifts of time, talent, and money, we have the supreme offering of Jesus in our mind's eye, and we are humbled. Amen.

Pastoral Prayer Pattern *(Passion Sunday)*

ONE: The cross lies clearly ahead for Jesus.

ALL: **The death of God's chosen one is reflected in those who suffer.**

ONE: Suffering as Jesus suffered, we pray for those who know they have a hard time of suffering ahead of them. *(time of silence)*

Suffering as Jesus suffered, we pray for those whose friends stayed away when they were needed most. *(time of silence)*

Suffering as Jesus suffered, we pray for those who overcome pressure and personal difficulty to stay beside their suffering friends.

Suffering as Jesus suffered, we pray for those who have kept to the moral high ground and who have suffered as a result.

The cross lies clearly ahead for Jesus.

ALL: **The death of God's chosen one is reflected in those who suffer.**

ONE: The cross lies clearly ahead for Jesus.

ALL: **The death of God's chosen one is reflected in those who suffer.**

ONE: We have made choices which have led to suffering.

We have experienced the loneliness that comes from taking the faithful path.

We have found comfort from unexpected people during the times that test us.

We have known the lowest point and God leading us away from that point.

The cross lies clearly ahead for Jesus.

ALL: **The death of God's chosen one is reflected in those who suffer.**

Commissioning *(Passion Sunday)*

ONE: We have seen Jesus struggling under the weight of the cross.

ALL: **Holy One, you will be with us in our struggles.**

ONE: We have seen Jesus insulted and mocked by soldiers and by leaders.

ALL: **Holy One, you will be with us when we are unjustly accused and ridiculed.**

ONE: We have seen Jesus trusted by the criminal bedside him.

ALL: **Holy One, we will trust you when the events of life leave us at a loss.**

ONE: We have seen Jesus faithfully followed by a group of brave women.

ALL: **Holy One, we will trust you when it is hard to persevere.**

Holy Thursday

Exodus 12:1–4, (5–10), 11–14
Psalm 116:1–2, 12–19
1 Corinthians 11:23–26
John 13:1–17, 31b–35

Jesus washes the disciples' feet

Call to Worship

ONE: People will understand your Christianity in the way you serve.

ALL: We will serve humbly; we will serve carefully.

ONE: People will notice your Christianity in the way you serve.

ALL: We will serve our loved ones, our family, and our friends.

ONE: People will notice your Christianity in the way you serve.

ALL: We will serve those in our faith community who need a boost.

ONE: People will notice your Christianity in the way you serve.

ALL: We will serve those in our neighbourhood who are going through hard times.

ONE: People will notice your Christianity in the way you serve.

ALL: We will serve the helpless and the despairing of other nations through our mission fund.

ONE: We have a leader and mentor in Jesus the Christ.

Opening Prayer

(Prior to the start of worship, place a towel and bowl on the communion table.)

ONE: We fill the bowl as we prepare to serve. *(Fill the bowl with water.)*
       We serve God through our worship.

ALL: **God is served as we pray, as we offer praise, as we listen to the Word, and as we discern what the Word is calling us to do.** *(Place towel beside the bowl.)*

ONE: We serve God as we care in a practical way for one another.

ALL: **God is served as we are alert to the needs of people in the church and as we meet those needs.**

ONE: We serve God as we search out those who are troubled and depressed.

ALL: **God is served as we stand with them and as we help them find empathetic support.**

ONE: We serve God as we accept the compassionate care of others.

ALL: **God is served as we receive graciously and give thanks generously. Amen.**

A Prayer of Remembering Jesus
(from 1 Corinthians 11:23–26)

ONE: Loving God,

ALL: **we gather as friends of Jesus at the communion table.**

ONE: He took the bread and gave thanks to God.

ALL: **We will take the bread, eat, and give God thanks for Jesus.**

ONE: He took the cup and spoke of the new covenant.

ALL: **We will take the cup and drink, for God remains faithful.**

ONE: We eat and drink and remember Jesus.

ALL: **We proclaim his life of service and his death on the cross.**

ONE: At the table, you are strengthened and encouraged as a faith community.

ALL: **From the table, we will go out to serve in the way of Jesus, a way of love.**

Words of Assurance

ONE: The bread brings us to give thanks.

ALL: **We have so much to give thanks for.** *(time of silent reflection)*

ONE: The wine reminds us of sacrifice.

ALL: **The faithful way of Jesus led to a cross.** *(time of silent reflection)*

ONE: Jesus has brought us to communion; we are strong together.

ALL: **In the church and in the world, we have his saving work to do.** *(time of silent reflection)*

ONE: Good News for today and tomorrow.

ALL: **We will proclaim the Good News in our words and by our actions. Amen.**

Offering Prayer

ONE: This is a place of offering, a place where God's people meet,

ALL: **to pray and to sing, to comfort one another and to remember.**

ONE: This is a place of offering, a place where God's people meet,

ALL: **to reflect and to be quiet, and to find opportunities for service.**

ONE: This is a holy space and you are God's holy people.

ALL: **God has blessed us in our gathering, and God will bless us as we go about the work of Jesus. Amen.**

Pastoral Prayer Pattern

ONE: Loving service, in bowl and towel, in bread and wine,

ALL: **we will serve faithfully.**

ONE: We will serve with our gifts refugees in squalid camps, and the homeless of this neighbourhood.
We will serve with our letters of support those languishing in prison and political prisoners.
We will serve by our advocacy children who are forced

to work and those who live with dementia.

We will serve with our presence family members in trouble and friends who have been bereaved.

Loving service, in bowl and towel, in bread and wine,

ALL: **we will serve faithfully.**

ONE: Loving service, in bowl and towel, in bread and wine,

ALL: **we will serve faithfully.**

ONE: These are the church friends we will serve: those who are housebound and those who are going through tough times.

These are the church friends we will serve: those who have needs we are able to meet, including the youngest who need activities and their parents who need support.

These are the church friends we will serve: people in our neighbourhood who need food and a place to sleep that is warm.

Loving service, in bowl and towel, in bread and wine,

ALL: **we will serve faithfully.**

Commissioning

ONE: Servants of the Holy One, you have work to do.

ALL: **We will meet to pray; Good Friday is coming close.**

We will meet to remember; the shadow of the cross hangs over us.

We will meet to listen; God will speak to us.

We will meet to find fresh resolve; tough tasks lie ahead for us,

We will meet in hope; Easter will change everything for us.

ONE: Servants of the Holy One, in all you do God will be your companion.

Go faithfully. Go in peace.

Good Friday

Isaiah 52:13 – 53:12

Psalm 22

Hebrews 10:16–25 – or Hebrews 4:14–16, 5:7–9

John 18:1 – 19:42

The arrest, trial, and crucifixion of Jesus

Call to Worship

ONE: Jesus, betrayed in the garden by his follower Judas –

ALL: crucifixion.

ONE: Jesus, denied in the High Priest's courtyard by his friend Peter –

ALL: crucifixion.

ONE: Jesus, questioned by the High Priest –

ALL: crucifixion.

ONE: Jesus examined by Pilate –

ALL: crucifixion.

ONE: Jesus, though innocent, sentenced to death –

ALL: crucifixion.

ONE: Jesus, condemned by a provoked crowd –

ALL: crucifixion.

ONE: Jesus, mocked by the soldiers –

ALL: crucifixion.

ONE: Jesus, hung on a cross beside two criminals –

ALL: crucifixion.

ONE: Jesus, suffering and dying, the women never left him –

ALL: crucifixion.

Opening Prayer

ONE: We approach the cross with sadness, loving God;

ALL: Jesus' teaching, helping, and healing, was cruelly ended.

ONE: We approach the cross with anger, loving God;

ALL: **the authorities abused their powe; a good man was killed.**

ONE: We approach the cross with surprise, loving God;

ALL: **his best friends, the twelve disciples, were afraid to stay with him.**

ONE: We approach the cross with humility, loving God;

ALL: **for the attitudes that brought Jesus to the cross-place are attitudes we share. Amen.**

or

ONE: When you ignore creative effort, or discourage fresh ways,

ALL: **look to the cross.**

ONE: When you are prepared to stand back when action is needed,

ALL: **look to the cross.**

ONE: When you are reluctant to stay with a person who needs support,

ALL: **look to the cross.**

ONE: When you encounter people who are out to get you,

ALL: **look to the cross.**

ONE: When you remember those who are loyal in the toughest times,

ALL: **give thanks and praise to God.** *(time of silent reflection)*

Words of Assurance

ONE: Create within us, loving God, a new spirit:

ALL: **a spirit that sings out with joy and longs to get involved,**
a spirit that refuses to blame and sees the best in others,
a spirit that is ready to give up self-satisfaction for the common good,
a spirit that is concerned for the truth,
a spirit that forgives even when it cannot forget,
a spirit that looks to Jesus for vitality and endurance.

ONE: Our loving God will create within you a new spirit.
       By the Holy Spirit, you will be renewed. Amen.

Offering Prayer

ONE: We see the cross. We see the cross and we give thanks
       to our loving God.

ALL: **We offer fellowship, we eat bread, we drink wine, and
       we remember Jesus.**

ONE: We see the cross.

ALL: **We offer church to those who are sick and to those
       who cannot worship with us.**

ONE: We see the cross.

ALL: **We offer support to Christians far beyond our shores.**

ONE: We see the cross.

ALL: **We offer the Good News to a world that needs the
       Good News so urgently.
       As we offer to God, so we are blessed. Amen.**

 ### Pastoral Prayer Pattern *(from John 18:37–38)*

ONE: Jesus was the truth-bringer, and the truth brought him
       to the cross.

ALL: **We will search diligently for the truth in our time; we
       will act on what we find.**

ONE: It is true that recent floods and smog are the direct
       result of more cars and increased industrialization.
       It is true that spending on the military is rising but
       many families still go without adequate food or
       housing.
       It is true that political prisoners are quickly forgotten,
       but letters written about them to national leaders will
       speed their release.
       It is true that in many companies the wages and
       salaries of women are lower than those of men, and
       there is no will to bring change.
       Jesus was the truth-bringer, and the truth brought him
       to the cross.

ALL: **We will search diligently for the truth in our time; we will act on what we find.**

ONE: Jesus was the truth-bringer, and the truth brought him to the cross.

ALL: **We will search diligently for the truth in our time; we will act on what we find.**

ONE: It is true that in many Indigenous communities water must be boiled before it can be drunk.
It is true that many children who have challenges in the classroom do not get the special help they need.
It is true that those who care for loved ones with dementias often do not receive adequate support.
It is true that for some medical procedures money can buy quicker diagnosis and treatment.
Jesus was the truth-bringer, and the truth brought him to the cross.

ALL: **We will search diligently for the truth in our time. We will act on what we find.**

Commissioning

ONE: Remember the cross of Jesus.

ALL: **When we are called to speak out for a just cause, we will remember.**

ONE: Remember the cross of Jesus.

ALL: **When we support friends who are in trouble, we will remember.**

ONE: Remember the cross of Jesus.

ALL: **When we see power and influence shamefully abused, we will remember.**

ONE: Remember the cross of Jesus.

ALL: **When we feel that we have cared enough, we will remember.**

ONE: Remember the cross of Jesus.

ALL: **For though he could have taken the easier way, Jesus stayed faithful to our loving God. We remember.**

Easter Sunday

Acts 10:34–43
> or Isaiah 65:17–25

Psalm 118:1–2, 14–24

1 Corinthians 15:19–26
> or Acts 10:34–43

John 20:1–18
> or Luke 24:1–12

The empty tomb... Jesus appears to Mary

Call to Worship

ONE: Death has been defeated!

ALL: **Welcome to new life in the risen Christ!**

ONE: Fear is overcome!

ALL: **Welcome to new life in the risen Christ!**

ONE: Loneliness is ended!

ALL: **Welcome to new life in the risen Christ!**

ONE: Hope replaces no-hope!

ALL: **Welcome to new life in the risen Christ!**

ONE: The powers are trembling!

ALL: **Welcome to new life in the risen Christ!**

ONE: The vulnerable are rejoicing!

ALL: **Welcome to new life in the risen Christ!**

ONE: Christ is risen!

ALL: **Christ is risen indeed!**

Opening Prayer

ONE: The word is out. "Jesus is risen," the best of all possible news.

"Jesus is risen!" Shout it from the housetops.

ALL: **The despairing will receive hope.**

ONE: "Jesus is risen!" Share it on social media.

ALL: **The downhearted will feel compassion.**

ONE: "Jesus is risen!" Make it known in the faith community.

ALL: **The shut-ins and sick will experience freedom.**

ONE: "Jesus is risen!" Broadcast it on radio and television.

ALL: **Those oppressed will break from tyranny's grip.**

ONE: "Jesus is risen!" We who are the people of Jesus

ALL: **will Alleluia it to our family and friends, and "Happy Easter!" the Good News to everyone we meet. In the name of the risen Christ we pray. Amen.**

Prayer: A New Creation *(from Isaiah 65:17–25)*

ONE: In the new creation, there is endless happiness.

ALL: **There is joy at the core of people just like us.**

ONE: In the new creation, people will be healthy and stay healthy.

ALL: **There will be no need to advocate exercise and a healthy diet; it will be the accepted way.**

ONE: Poor housing, cold rooms, water that must be boiled, will not exist.

ALL: **The need for warm and homely accommodation will be met for every single person and family.**

ONE: Flowers and animals will be accepted as precious in God's sight.

ALL: **Pets will be enjoyed and protected.**

ONE: Work will be fulfilling, create good relationships, and be fun.

ALL: **For those who want to work, jobs will always be available.**

ONE: Men and women will live to a ripe old age,

ALL: **and all children will be cherished and protected.**

ONE: Our Easter hope is that God's new creation is on the way.

ALL: **We will bring closer its wonderful order on this vulnerable planet of ours.** *(time of silent reflection)*

Words of Assurance

ONE: Take heart, those of you who worry about acid rain.
Take heart, those of you who are concerned about the
endless stream of refugees.
Take heart, those of you who see the conflicts of our
world and despair.
Take heart those of you who see discrimination
because of race.

ALL: **It is our Easter hope that change will happen.
God has given us the vision. God has shown God's
commitment to us and our world in Jesus. We have
nothing to fear.**

ONE: You are God's way to bring change, one person, one
corner of God's world at a time.
Go to work!

ALL: **We will work in the way of Christ.
We will work joyfully in the Spirit. Amen.**

Offering Prayer

ONE: Loving God, accept our gifts, given to bring a flourish
of new life on this Easter Sunday.

ALL: **May our children laugh and sing. May our "oldsters"
join with them.
May our leaders respond to the challenges and may
our families find friends.**

ONE: May our instrumentalists and choir love their music,
and our minister and worship leaders love the Word
just as much.

ALL: **May we go into our neighbourhood with enthusiasm
and stand with the troubled. May we meet the needs of
the wider world through our mission fund.**

ONE: We are glad we can give and glad that our offering will
be well-used.
We pray in the name of the risen Christ.

ALL: **Amen.**

Pastoral Prayer Pattern *(from Luke 24:1–12)*

ONE: Fear, surprise, amazement.

ALL: **The astounding news, Jesus is risen:**

ONE: risen to proclaim that suffering can be overcome in every corner of the world;

risen to proclaim that the powerful can no longer keep health and healing from the poorest and the most at risk;

risen to proclaim that we can find a way to support those who we know are going through testing times. We pray for our family members and members of our church family;

risen to proclaim that those we know who have lost loved ones can come gently out of the tomb of bereavement.

ONE: Fear, surprise, amazement –

ALL: **the astounding news, Jesus is risen!**

ONE: Faith is alive to inspire our church family to serve enthusiastically.

Faith is alive to support mission work globally,

Faith is alive to touch the most vulnerable immediately.

Faith is alive to banish apathy absolutely.

Fear, surprise, amazement –

ALL: **the astounding news, Jesus is risen!**

Commissioning

ONE: Go out as an Easter people, rejoicing in Jesus risen, ready to bring new life closer.

ALL: **Sing out God's praises, have done with apathy.**

ONE: Comfort the faint-hearted; fill them with courage.

ALL: **Speak out for the refugee; find work for the newcomer.**

ONE: Care for the challenged ones; stay beside the down-hearted.

ALL: **Accept help graciously.**

ONE: Listen carefully.

ALL: **God has work for us to do. As Easter people, we will take our discipleship seriously.**

2nd Sunday of Easter

Acts 5:27–32
Psalm 118:14–29
             or Psalm 150
Revelation 1:4–8
John 20:19–31

Jesus is with the disciples and brings peace

Call to Worship

ONE: This is God's promise!
ALL: **New life is ours; Jesus is risen!**
ONE: This is our living hope!
ALL: **New life is ours; Jesus is risen!**
ONE: More precious than a fortune!
ALL: **New life is ours; Jesus is risen!**
ONE: A faith that will endure!
ALL: **New life is ours; Jesus is risen!**
ONE: A great and glorious joy!
       New life is ours; Jesus is risen!

Opening Prayer

ONE: We come to God with questions.
ALL: **Living God, you welcome our questions.**
ONE: We come to God with doubts.
ALL: **Living God you welcome our doubts.**
ONE: We come to God with unbelief.
ALL: **Living God, you turn our unbelief to faith.**
ONE: We come to God, not sure to whom we should turn.
ALL: **You show us Jesus risen, the source of our peace.
Amen.**

Prayer of Easter Transformation

ONE: Jesus is risen!
Jesus alive transforms our life and the life of our faith community.

ALL: **Where there was apathy now there is action.**

ONE: Jesus is risen!

ALL: **Where there was doubt now there is faith.**

ONE: Jesus is risen!

ALL: **Where there was exclusion, now we count all people our sisters and brothers.**

ONE: Jesus is risen!

ALL: **Where there was avoidance of issues, now there is responsibility.**

ONE: Jesus is risen!

ALL: **Where there was darkness and uncertainty, now there is hope.**

ONE: Jesus is risen!

ALL: **Where there were limits of time and space, now the limits are at an end.** *(time of silent reflection)*

Prayer of Easter Assurance

ONE: Thanks be to God, our doubts are behind us,

ALL: **and we hear the words, "Peace be with you."**

ONE: Thanks be to God, our failures and our shortcomings are forgiven,

ALL: **and we hear the words, "Peace be with you."**

ONE: Thanks be to God, our dreams are now possibilities,

ALL: **and we hear the words, "Peace be with you."**

ONE: Thanks be to God, we can do the work that Jesus Christ began,

ALL: **and we hear the words, "Peace be with you." Thanks be to God. Amen.**

Offering Prayer

ONE: In our giving, for those of our faith community who are sick and troubled,

ALL: **we bring peace.**
ONE: In our giving, to provide time and space for prayer and meditation,
ALL: **we bring peace.**
ONE: In our giving, to bring people together for praise and reflection on the Word,
ALL: **we bring peace.**
ONE: In our giving, to break down the barriers that keep hatred and suspicion alive,
ALL: **we bring peace.**
ONE: In our giving, to help those whose names we will never know,
ALL: **we bring peace.**
ONE: Our giving is blessed with peace.
ALL: **Thanks be to God. Amen**

 Pastoral Prayer Pattern

ONE: In your believing, in your questioning, praise God!
ALL: **God's love is eternal.**
ONE: A good question: Can our planet sustain the present level of carbon dioxide that is poisoning the atmosphere?
A good question: will there be no end to the suffering of children and old people forced to become refugees?
A good question: can trade barriers be broken down so that the poorest are able to trade with the richest nations?
A good question: will health care be available to each member of planet Earth, wherever they live and however scarce their resources?
In your believing, in your questioning, praise God!
ALL: **God's love is eternal.**

ONE: In your believing, in your questioning, praise God!

ALL: **God's love is eternal.**

ONE: We will praise God in the freedom that is ours to
       question the creeds and to interpret scripture.
       We will praise God in the freedom that is ours to go
       outside the conventional ways of worship, praise, and
       prayer.
       We will praise God in the freedom that is ours to learn
       from other faith groups and from their sacred
       scriptures.
       In your believing, in your questioning, praise God!

ALL: **God's love is eternal.**

Commissioning

ONE: Followers, pick your leaders carefully.

ALL: **Waverers, find commitment.**

ONE: Strugglers, know peace.

ALL: **Doubters, persist in questioning.**

ONE: Wanderers, find the Way.

ALL: **Believers, rejoice in Jesus Christ.**

3rd Sunday of Easter

Acts 9:1–6, (7–20)
Psalm 30
Revelation 5:11–14
John 21:1–19

Jesus appears on the lakeshore...a huge catch of fish

Call to Worship

ONE: You come to us, living God.

ALL: **You come to us in the still, small voice, and we listen.**

ONE: You come to us, living God.

ALL: **You come to us in a flash of insight, and we are amazed.**

ONE: You come to us, living God.

ALL: **You come to us when we least expect you, and we are surprised.**

ONE: You come to us, living God.

ALL: **You come to us in these moments of worship, and we rejoice.**

Opening Prayer *(from John 21:1–14)*

ONE: Loving God, we thank you for the lakeshore Jesus.

ALL: **Jesus stands on the shore; in the sunlight he is hard to recognize.**

ONE: We thank you for the questioning Jesus.

ALL: **Jesus asks us about our progress and shows how we can turn failure into success.**

ONE: We thank you for the "outside the box" thinking Jesus.

ALL: **Jesus encourages us to try a way we have never tried before.**

ONE: We thank you for Jesus who feeds his disciples.

ALL: **Following the words and work of Jesus fulfills us beyond all expectations.**

Loving God, we thank you for the lakeshore teacher. Amen.

or

ONE: Holy One, you amaze us with your presence.

ALL: **When we least expect it, you are among us.**

ONE: You amaze us with your presence.

ALL: **When we are discouraged, you give us hope.**

ONE: You amaze us with your presence.

ALL: **When we are frustrated, you bring us peace.**

ONE: You amaze us with your presence.

ALL: **When we are out of ideas, you inspire us.**

ONE: You amaze us with your presence.

ALL: **When we receive the help we need, we experience you in friend and stranger.**

ONE: We thank you, amazing God.

ALL: **Amen.**

A Prayer of Pastoral Caring

ONE: Loving God, you call us to a ministry of compassion. Open our eyes to the needs of family and friends.

ALL: **How can we support and encourage those closest to us?** *(time of silent reflection)*

ONE: Show us the ways we can help church family members.

ALL: **How can we support and encourage members of our own faith community?** *(time of silent reflection)*

ONE: Alert us to those who are troubled, and to those lacking shelter and food in our local community.

ALL: **How can we support them and meet basic needs?** *(time of silence)*

ONE: Confront us with refugees, the starving, and political prisoners, our worldwide sisters and brothers.

ALL: **How can we support those whom war has scarred, leaders have abused, and conflict has rendered poor and homeless?** *(time of silent reflection)*

A Prayer of Compassion

ONE: Compassion calls us to love as we have been loved by you, most gracious God:

ALL: **to love those who love us and those who reject us;**
to love those whom we like and those whom we do not like;
to love those whose story we have heard first hand, and those whose story comes to us second hand;
to love those with needs who are on our street, and those whose home is an ocean away;
to love those who are Christian and those who are Muslim, and Sikh, and Buddhist.

ONE: It is the compassion of the risen Christ that calls us to love without limits.

ALL: **We recognize that this love is neither easy to give nor to receive. Amen.**

Offering Prayer

ONE: You call us, O God, to give care-fully, generously, even extravagantly to advance the life pattern of Christ in this faith community, and wherever our mission fund reaches.

ALL: **We give our money and you will bless it.**
We give our time and you will hallow it.
We give our recognized talents and you remind us.
We have more talents to discover.

ONE: Receive these gifts and our wholehearted commitment to Jesus, whom we follow with joy. Amen.

💔 Pastoral Prayer Pattern

ONE: Powerful change for good, the Easter experience,

ALL: **and we will help it happen.**

ONE: Political leaders will see the needs of troubled schoolchildren, and provide more support for them. Those addicted to opioids will be contacted and will have access to rehabilitation groups.

Lonely youngsters will know where to go for friendship and will put their fears aside.

Elderly people with dementia will find support programs, and their caregivers will find respite.

Powerful change for good, the Easter experience,

ALL: **and we will help it happen.**

ONE: Powerful change for good, the Easter experience,

ALL: **and we will know it for ourselves:**

ONE: our apathy faced and replaced with positive decisions, our use of time considered and new priorities worked out,

our poor relationships admitted and action taken to improve or end them,

our self-interest recognized and the needs of others met.

Powerful change for good, the Easter experience,

ALL: **and we will know it for ourselves.**

Commissioning

ONE: God will meet us when and where we least expect God to be.

ALL: **God meets us with faith in our times of doubt.**

God meets us with strength when we feel weak.

God meets us with fresh enthusiasm when we feel disillusioned.

God meets us with hope in deepest despair.

God meets us with joy at our moments of sadness.

And we know the spirit of the risen Christ in our midst!

4th Sunday of Easter

Acts 9:36–43
Psalm 23
Revelation 7:9–17
John 10:22–30

God is our shepherd... Jesus is rejected

Call to Worship *(from Psalm 23)*

ONE: You give us everything we need, O God.

ALL: **We shall not want.**

ONE: God calms us; God restores our souls.

ALL: **We shall not want.**

ONE: In the darkest times,

ALL: **we shall not want.**

ONE: When we are lost,

ALL: **we shall not want.**

ONE: In times of danger,

ALL: **we shall not want.**

ONE: In the best of times,

ALL: **we shall not want.**

ONE: At the time of death and beyond,

ALL: **we shall not want.**

ONE: For you, living God, give us everything we need.

Opening Prayer

ONE: We hear your voice, living God, and we listen,

ALL: **as sheep hear the voice of their shepherd and respond.**

ONE: We hear your voice through the words and deeds of Jesus,

ALL: **challenging words and acts of compassion.**

ONE: We hear your voice through good words and just acts of Christians today,

ALL: **and we too will speak out and follow courageously.**

ONE: We know that we may be misunderstood,

ALL: **but we will speak out directly and clearly.**

ONE: We know that rejection is a possibility,

ALL: **but we will persevere.**

ONE: Nothing in this life can touch us, nothing can overcome us,

ALL: **for you, loving God, are with us and are eternally to be trusted. Amen.**

or

ONE: When you are around, shepherd God,

ALL: **we will have everything we need.**

ONE: The shepherd God says, "Take it easy,"

ALL: **and we will relax.**

ONE: The shepherd God says, "Follow me,"

ALL: **and we know we are going in the right direction.**

ONE: The shepherd God says, "In the darkest moment I am there,"

ALL: **and we will take courage.**

ONE: The shepherd God says, "You can sit down and eat with your enemies,"

ALL: **and we will know your reassuring presence.**

ONE: The shepherd God says, "In time and beyond time, I am there,"

ALL: **and we will be confident and strong.**

ONE: When you are around, shepherd God,

ALL: **we will have everything we need. Amen.**

A Prayer of Testing

ONE: Jesus, God's anointed one, tests our faithfulness.

ALL: **Are we able and willing to clearly state our beliefs?** *(time of silent reflection)*

ONE: Jesus, God's anointed one, tests our courage.

ALL: **Are we able and willing to go against the commonly held views of the crowd?** *(time of silent reflection)*

ONE: Jesus, God's anointed one, tests our tenacity.

ALL: **Are we able and willing to resist when the pressure is on?** *(time of silent reflection)*

ONE: Jesus, God's anointed one, tests our trust.

ALL: **Are we able and willing to follow the Good Shepherd when the way ahead is neither certain nor smooth?** *(time of silent reflection)*

Assurance that God Is Trustworthy

ONE: God will not let you down.

ALL: **In the hardest situations, God's love is there for us.**

ONE: God will not let you down.

ALL: **When good friends find reasons to stay away, God's love is near and dear to us.**

ONE: God will not let you down.

ALL: **When our values are neither accepted nor appreciated, God's love shines through.**

ONE: God will not let you down.

ALL: **When our time merges with God's limitless time, we will trust God.**

ONE: God will not let you down; God's love is here today, and in all the days to come, God's love will be.

ALL: **Amen.**

Offering Prayer

ONE: These gifts are presented so that the Good Shepherd will be known, accepted and followed. They are life-changing, world-shaking gifts:

ALL: **gifts worked out as compassion spreads through this faith community,**
gifts worked out as the Word is preached and Christian work is encouraged,
gifts worked out as people find confidence and use fresh talents,
gifts worked out through the inspiring projects of our mission fund.

ONE: Living God, bless these gifts and us the givers, in the name of Jesus Christ who gave extravagantly in life and in his cross-death.

ALL: **Amen.**

or

Offering Prayer *(from John 10:22–39)*

ONE: Jesus was rejected, but stayed faithful.

ALL: **Our gifts are gifts from the faithful.**
Faithfully we will offer praise and prayer.
Faithfully we will serve within this faith community.
We will serve the young and questioning.
We will serve the infirm and struggling.
We will serve the troubled and we will celebrate with the joyful.
Faithfully we will serve those who are helped by our mission fund.
In faithful service, our gifts will go to work, and you, living God, will bless them. Amen.

 ### Pastoral Prayer Pattern *(from John 10:22–39)*

ONE: Rejection is hard to endure.

ALL: **Loving God, we stand with the despised and rejected.**

ONE: The powerful ones find it difficult to regulate the effects of polluting the atmosphere.
We stand with those who protest.
The homeless ask for basic housing that will provide security and warmth.
We stand with them.
Mothers with small children search for affordable daycare; politicians say it is too expensive.
We stand with the mothers.
International aid organizations make clear the need for more funds to give permanent homes for refugees; few respond.
We stand with the aid organizations.
Rejection is hard to endure.

ALL: **Loving God, we stand with the despised and rejected.**

ONE: Rejection is hard to endure.

ALL: **Loving God, we stand with the despised and rejected.**

ONE: Many Indigenous people live in conditions that are unsanitary, unhealthy, and cold.

ALL: **We will advocate for them.**

ONE: *We who are Indigenous live without water that is drinkable and without access to higher education. It is hard to make our voices heard.*

Refugees and new immigrants find it hard to learn English or French, and to hold down a job to sustain their families in the new country.

ALL: **We will support them.**

ONE: *We who are newcomers are trying hard to come to terms with the prevailing culture. It is tough to stand in the margins in our homeland culture, and in this one.*

Rejection is hard to endure

ALL: **Loving God, we stand with the despised and rejected.**

Commissioning

ONE: Are you ready to follow the Good Shepherd faithfully?

ALL: **We are ready.**

ONE: Are you ready to stand up to the easy-going crowd?

ALL: **We are ready.**

ONE: Are you ready to speak out boldly?

ALL: **We are ready.**

ONE: Are you ready to act for the just way?

ALL: **We are ready.**

ONE: Are you ready to speak and act with this faith community?

ALL: **We are ready.**

ONE: God's blessing is yours. You *are* ready.

5th Sunday of Easter

sometimes celebrated as Christian Family Sunday

Acts 11:1–18
Psalm 148
Revelation 21:1–6
John 13:31–35

An inclusive dream with consequences

Call to Worship
(appropriate people might offer this prayer)

ONE: Count us in, loving God;

ALL: **some of us have come on skateboards to church.**

ONE: Count us in, loving God;

ALL: **some of us have come by bike and by car.**

ONE: Count us in, loving God;

ALL: **some of us have wheeled and some used walkers.**

ONE: Count us in, loving God;

ALL: **some of us are feeling just great, and some of us low and in pain.**

ONE: Count us in, loving God;

ALL: **some of us have questions to ask, and some of us want faithful certainty.**

ONE: Count us in, loving God;

ALL: **some of us are here to sing and pray, and some of us to reflect on the Word.**

ONE: However we come, whatever our concerns, you welcome us, you accept us, and you, O God, love us without reservation;

ALL: **and we rejoice in our worship.**

Opening Prayer

ONE: At the centre, at the core of the Holy One, love:

ALL: **a love that can never be overcome.**

ONE: At the centre of compassion, love:

ALL: **a love rooted in caring and healing.**

ONE: At the centre of justice, love:

ALL: **sworn enemy of bullying and control.**

ONE: At the centre of faith, love:

ALL: **a love that is patterned in the life of Jesus.**

ONE: As Paul the apostle wrote;

ALL: **"Love bears all things, believes all things, hopes all things, endures all things. Love never ends." Amen.**

A Prayer for Family Sunday

(participation by significant congregational members)

ONE: I'm on my own and have few, though caring family members.

ALL: **God rejoices you are here.**

ONE: Our family has lots of children, countess cousins.

ALL: **God rejoices you are here.**

ONE: I have grandchildren I love, grandchildren who visit me.

ALL: **God rejoices you are here.**

ONE: I have a sister, *Rachael, who is four, and a beautiful dog called Rover.*

ALL: **God rejoices you are here.**

ONE: I'm *June,* and I'm *Judy* and we have each other and a very intelligent cat called *Pepper.*

ALL: **God rejoices you are here. And we all rejoice that you who offer prayer are here, and that we have our church family to support and sustain us. Amen.**

A Prayer of Inclusion

ONE: No one will be excluded.

ALL: **Those who are black or white, or any rainbow shade, we include you in.**

ONE: No one will be excluded.

ALL: **Those who are gay or straight, lesbian or transgendered or queer, we include you in.**

ONE: No one will be excluded.

ALL: **Those who are rich or poor, with much education or with much common sense, we include you in.**

ONE: No one will be excluded.

ALL: **Christian or Jew, Muslim or Hindu, Sikh or Buddhist, we include all faiths in.**

ONE: In our places of worship, in our cultural centres, in our community centres, in our centres of government,

ALL: **you call us, living God, to be advocates for inclusion, and confronters of prejudice, as Jesus was.** *(time of silent reflection)*

A Prayer for the Strength to Include

ONE: Living God, when we find ourselves judging or comparing, ranking or criticizing, show us the way of Jesus.

ALL: **Jesus gave women an equal place in a male-dominated society.**
Jesus showed the worth of poor people where the rich were powerful leaders.
Jesus showed compassion to foreigners.
Jesus showed the importance of children.
Jesus showed the value of those who were ready to forgive.

ONE: Are we ready to do the same?

ALL: **Amen.**

Offering Prayer
(use petitions that fit your own situation)

ONE: Our gifts are lovingly given; accept them, O God.

ALL: **With these gifts, we can worship Sunday by Sunday.**
With these gifts, we can play with and teach children and young people.

With these gifts, we can support the sick and struggling ones.
With these gifts, we can promote justice.

ONE: Our gifts are lovingly given to support our local community.

ALL: **With these gifts, we can help *the food bank,***
With these gifts, we can provide space *for Alcoholics Anonymous* to meet.

ONE: Our gifts are lovingly given to support the mission life of our church.

ALL: **With these gifts, we enable *Syrian* refugees to find a home.**
With these gifts, we enable inner city youth to prepare for job search.

ONE: You give lovingly, and in return you receive God's Spirit joyfully.

ALL: **We give thanks. Amen.**

💔 Pastoral Prayer Pattern

ONE: Jesus loved beyond the limits of his time and place.

ALL: **Loving God, we are called to include the excluded of our time.**

ONE: Where those with physically challenges cannot enter a restaurant, a church, or a bathroom, we are called to inclusion.
Where children with Attention Deficit Disorder are ignored or disciplined, we are called to speak up for them.
Where elderly people with infirmities are treated without due compassion or care, we are called to speak out.
Where our shut-in church members are forgotten, we are called to remember.
Jesus loved beyond the limits of his time and place.

ALL: **Loving God, we are called to include the excluded of our time.**

ONE: Jesus loved beyond the limits of his time and place.

ALL: Loving God, each one of us prays to be included.

ONE: When we cannot feel acceptance in a social group,

ALL: we pray to be included.

ONE: When we silently cry out for friendship but are
     ignored,

ALL: we pray to be included.

ONE: When we are talked down to or are patronized,

ALL: we pray to be included.

ONE: Where we lack the skills we need for an essential task,

ALL: we pray to be included.

ONE: Jesus loved beyond the limits of his time and place.

**ALL: Loving God, we are called to include the excluded of
     our time, and we pray for inclusion.**

Commissioning

ONE: Share generously the love that God has given you. It is
     a powerful, relevant love.

**ALL: Where self-serving rules, love will speak of giving, not
     receiving.
     Where people are hurting, love will stand patiently
     beside them.
     Where injustice is reality, love will call out for a
     different response.
     Where discrimination is found, love will insist on
     acceptance.
     Where death or loss is present, love will listen and
     direct towards new life.**

ONE: Love is powerful. Share generously the love that God
     has given you.

6th Sunday of Easter

Acts 16:9–15
Psalm 67
Revelation 21:10, 22 – 22:5
John 14:23–29
   or John 5:1–9

Lydia hears about Jesus ...a healing miracle... the Holy Spirit is the peace bringer

Call to Worship *(from Psalm 67)*

ONE: God be gracious to us and bless us.
ALL: **May the light of God shine upon us.**
ONE: God's Way is the way for our world.
ALL: **God's salvation can change the nations for good.**
ONE: Everyone will praise our God.
ALL: **People everywhere will praise God's name.**
ONE: Nations will be glad and sing for joy.
ALL: **For God' way will change the world for good.**
ONE: Everyone will praise our God.
ALL: **People everywhere will praise God's name.**
ONE: For God has blessed us abundantly.
ALL: **God will continue to bless us.**

Opening Prayer *(from Acts 16:9–15)*

ONE: We come to listen to your Word, O God.
ALL: **We rejoice that we are here.**
ONE: We come to pray and to sing.
ALL: **We rejoice in this hour of worship.**
ONE: We come and are open to your Word for each one of us.
ALL: **We rejoice in new insights and fresh ways.**
ONE: We believe that you have a word for our family and for our friends.

We believe you have a word for our faith community.

ALL: **We rejoice as we hear the Good News, share the Good News, and put the Good News to work.**

ONE: You have come with anticipation; you will go out with heartfelt joy.

ALL: **Thanks be to God. Amen.**

A Prayer Recognizing the Peace of Christ

ONE: Into our uncertainty and confusion,

ALL: **the Spirit breathes the peace of Christ.** *(time of silent reflection)*

ONE: Into our doubting and questioning,

ALL: **the Spirit breathes the peace of Christ.** *(time of silent reflection)*

ONE: Into our broken relationships, our distance from another,

ALL: **the Spirit breathes the peace of Christ.** *(time of silent reflection)*

ONE: Into the challenging areas of our faith community,

ALL: **the Spirit breathes the peace of Christ.** *(time of silent reflection)*

ONE: Into our anxiety about new endeavours, changing dreams into action,

ALL: **the Spirit breathes the peace of Christ.** *(time of silent reflection)*

The Gift of Peace

ONE: Jesus says, "Peace I leave with you; my peace I give to you. Not as the world gives do I give to you. Do not let your hearts be troubled, neither let them be afraid."

ALL: **We receive the gift of peace, the gift of the Holy Spirit. Amen.**

Offering Prayer

ONE: We bring our very practical gifts – money, time, and talents – for use in ways of the Spirit.

ALL: **We will use our gifts to gather for worship the old and the young, the happy and the discouraged, and those abled in different ways.**

ONE: These gifts will be heard in our singing and will enable our silent waiting.

ALL: **We will use our gifts to learn about the way of Jesus for our time.**

We will use our gifts to build up the faith community in this place.

We will use our gifts globally to help those without hope and without a home.

ONE: In the Spirit, our gifts will be blessed beyond imagining.

ALL: **Amen.**

 ## Pastoral Prayer Pattern

ONE: Into our troubled world comes the Holy Spirit.

ALL: **We rejoice, for the Spirit shows the way to peace.**

ONE: The Spirit gives hope to those who have left their homeland and family because they were in mortal danger… *(refugee situation)*.

The Spirit motivates those who are starting new businesses, new ventures.

The Spirit confronts employers who exploit their workers… *(contemporary situation)*.

The Spirit will not rest until all nuclear and chemical weapons are destroyed.

The Spirit welcomes our political action to make the world a safer, healthier place.

Into our troubled world comes the Holy Spirit.

ALL: **We rejoice, for the Spirit shows the way to peace.**

ONE: Into our troubled world comes the Holy Spirit.

ALL: **We rejoice, for the Spirit shows the way to peace.**

ONE: The Spirit actively works with the members of very

different faith groups to promote unity of action.
The Spirit encourages faith community members to use new skills and talents in Christ's service.
The Spirit is with our family members who are searching for a faith path that is relevant for them.
The Spirit refuses to give up when our faith is tested.
Into our troubled world comes the Holy Spirit.

ALL: **We rejoice, for the Spirit shows the way to peace.**

Commissioning

ONE: Go from this church Spirit-filled and Spirit-led.

ALL: **The Spirit will remind us of all we have achieved on our Christian journey.
The Spirit will encourage us as we go about our daily work and leisure.
The Spirit will be with us in all the months and years that lie ahead, a source of joy, a source of inspiration, a source of peace:**

ONE: God's peace, a peace that passes all human understanding. Amen.

7th Sunday of Easter

Acts 16:16–34
Psalm 97
Revelation 22:12–14, 16–17, 20–21
John 17:20–26

"So they may be one as we are one"

Call to Worship *(from Psalm 97)*

ONE: Grant us, living God, a vision of your glory come to earth, a vision of your glory for every nation and people.

ALL: **Its foundation is moral rightness, compassion, and justice for all.**

ONE: Nothing can stand in the path of God's loving power.

ALL: **Self-serving and the worship of money or position will be at an end.**

ONE: It will no longer be the corrupt politicians and leaders who can be manipulated who will dominate.

ALL: **Those who are in tune with God's long-term loving way will overcome and will be universally recognized.**

ONE: Evildoers will be exposed and rooted out, and the faithful ones will energize the governments of the nations.

ALL: **Rejoice, all of you who are with God, and give thanks to God's holy name.**

Opening Prayer

ONE: A cry from the heart, a cry for unity, "That they may all be one."
Unity as we worship:

ALL: **we bring our different talents to church, our different gifts, opinions, and practices.**

ONE: Unity in the family of Jesus Christ:

ALL: **we sing different hymns, pray different prayers, but we all gather round the communion table, read the same Word, and fight the same injustice and poverty.**

ONE: Unity as members of the global village:

ALL: **we live in bitter cold and in tropical heat, but we are united as we give hope to refugees and fight the starvation of children.**

ONE: Unity as one faith group among others:

ALL: **we are ready to listen to the beliefs of others, to read their sacred scriptures, and to work together with them for the good of humanity.**

ONE: A cry from the heart, a cry from the church, a cry for unity,

ALL: **"That they may all be one." Amen.**

Striving for Unity

ONE: A cry from the heart, a cry for unity, "That they may all be one."

Unity within the family circle:

ALL: **not a superficial unity where issues are brushed aside and old grudges go unmentioned, but a deep listening, and a willingness to forgive.** *(time of silent reflection)*

ONE: Unity within the faith community:

ALL: **not a superficial unity where leaders get what they want, but a worked-through unity where all are consulted and the opinions of children and those advanced in years are taken to heart.** *(time of silent reflection)*

ONE: Unity between faith communities:

ALL: **not a superficial unity, where differences are hidden and politeness veils deep divisions, but an open prayerful willingness, a willingness to let the Holy Spirit speak of all we share.** *(time of silent reflection)*

ONE: Unity between nations:

ALL: **not a superficial unity where old hostilities are masked and exist unmentioned, but a true meeting of minds**

where challenges are worked through and visions are
shared. *(time of silent reflection)*

Assurance of a Fresh Start

ONE: God does not blame or condemn. God seeks to make
clear the realities, initiate fresh visions, and inspire
new starts.

ALL: **We will prayerfully trust God to lead us towards the
unity we seek in our personal lives, within and between
faith communities, and in our troubled and needy
world. Amen.**

Offering Prayer

ONE: These gifts bring people together to glorify God, and
to be about Gods' work in this time and place.

ALL: **Loving God, you bless our gifts and our giving, and
your love binds us together.
Bring us together to praise and to pray.
Bring us together to learn and to teach.
Bring us together to share the pattern of Christ with
our friends, our *town*, and our world.
Bring us together as a faith community to do justice, to
love kindness, and to walk humbly with you, our loving
God. Amen.**

Pastoral Prayer Pattern

ONE: God's glory in our world, our church, our humanity:

ALL: **we will work to show God's glory.**

ONE: We will work to keep God's creation good: the rivers
clean, the earth fertile, the air of the cities pure.
We will work to break down the barriers between
nations and to put smiles on the faces of the
downhearted.
We will work to free the political prisoners and to
speak out for the voiceless.
We will work to bring self-respect to the despised and

to affirm the worth of those who are struggling.
God's glory in our world, our church, our humanity:

ALL: **we will work to show God's glory.**

ONE: God's glory in our world, our church in our humanity:
ALL: **we will work to show God's glory.**
ONE: Where all are welcomed warmly, God's glory is there.
Where young and old are given a chance to lead,
God's glory is there.
In a reaching out with other faith groups to meet the
needs of our town, God's glory is there.
In a common exploration of the scriptures, God's glory
is there.
God's glory in our world, our church, our humanity:
ALL: **we will work to show God's glory.**

Commissioning

ONE: Go from here as those who seek to promote unity.
ALL: **We will work to bring friends and family members
together.
We will work to banish fear and put-downs and hate.
We will work to make our church a beacon of hope in
this neighbourhood.
We will work to encourage different Christian groups
as they go about joint compassionate projects.
We will work to provide a home to those who can no
longer return to their traditional home.
We will work as those who care deeply about our
planet.
We will work to counter the effects of global warming.**
ONE: In your work with others, God goes with you; God's
vision is clearly ahead of you.

Pentecost Sunday

Acts 2:1–21
> or Genesis 11:1–9

Psalm 104:24–34, 35b

Romans 8:14–17
> or John 14:8–17, (25–27)

The coming of the Holy Spirit

Call to Worship

ONE: Come celebrate the birthday of the church.

ALL: **We remember the first Christians gathered in the power of the Spirit.**

ONE: Come celebrate the birthday of the church.

ALL: **We rejoice in the power of love that has marked the faithful church down the ages.**

ONE: Come celebrate the birthday of the church.

ALL: **We welcome the challenge that comes today through the lively Spirit.**

ONE: Come celebrate the birthday of the church.

ALL: **We will respond with words that enlighten and acts of compassion.**

Opening Prayer *(from John 14:17)*

ONE: The Spirit of truth invites us to worship;

ALL: **in prayer, in praise, and in the silence, we are inspired.**

ONE: The Spirit of truth calls us to listen,

ALL: **and the Word of our Loving God speaks quietly to us.**

ONE: The Spirit of truth confronts the lies and distortions,

ALL: **and shows us the just and merciful way.**

ONE: The Spirit of truth arises from the life of Jesus,

ALL: **and challenges us to the opportunity and the joy of discipleship. Amen.**

A Prayer of Communication

ONE: Spirit of life, we rejoice that we can speak together, sing together, and laugh together.

ALL: **Where we will not speak to another, prefer solos over choruses, and keep a poker face, forgive us.**

ONE: Spirit of life, we rejoice that we can use texting, email, and Facetime to keep in touch with friends and loved ones.

ALL: **Where we avoid personal meetings and greetings, forgive us.**

ONE: Spirit of life, we admit that we turn back at the barrier of language and miss the need, the experience, or the culture of another.

ALL: **Where we have failed to understand the joys or sorrows of culturally different people, forgive us.**

ONE: Spirit of life, we are thankfully amazed at the variety of faith and religious practice that we encounter.

ALL: **Where we will not explore the holy books and listen to the wise elders of other faith groups, forgive us.** *(time of silent reflection)*

Assurance of Understanding

ONE: Spirit of life, you call us to communication:

ALL: **to break down the barriers of attitude and language; to use all media, speech, and skill to show our compassion; to work faithfully with people we know and with others different in culture and approach, to bring peace; to cooperate with caring people of all nations to safeguard the life of our planet.**

ONE: Spirit of life, you will inspire and surprise us.

ALL: **Thank you. Amen.**

Offering Prayer

ONE: We love our church.

ALL: **We will support the work our church carries out in the name of Jesus Christ.**

ONE: Within this faith community,

ALL: **our gifts promote healing and counter loneliness.**

ONE: Within this faith community,

ALL: **our gifts encourage youngsters and support the housebound.**

ONE: Through our mission fund,

ALL: **our gifts train young people and enable women and girls to provide for themselves.**

ONE: We love our church and we are prepared to give,

ALL: **but in giving we also receive. Amen.**

Pastoral Prayer Pattern *(from Romans 8:4–18)*

ONE: The Spirit is with all who suffer. To those who are going through times of challenge, listen.

ALL: **The Spirit is with you, don't be afraid.**

ONE: The Spirit is with those who have received worrying news this week.
       The Spirit is with those whose recovery is painfully slow.
       The Spirit is with those who have suffered a setback in health or in the progress of life. *(time of silent reflection)*
       The Spirit is with those who are having difficulty sleeping or eating. *(time of silent reflection)*
       The Spirit is with those who have lost a loved one.
       The Spirit is with those burdened by grief. *(time of silent reflection)*
       The Spirit is with you.

ALL: **Don't be afraid.**

ONE: The Spirit is with you.

ALL: **Don't be afraid.**

ONE: In the relationships that are stressed, the Spirit is with us.
       In our moments of doubt and despair, the Spirit is with us.

When friends let us down, the Spirit is with us.
When we shrink back from the faithful action, the
Spirit is with us.
When we fill our life with too many people or things,
the Spirit is with us. *(time of silent reflection)*
The Spirit is with you.

ALL: **We will not be afraid.**

Commissioning

ONE: Go from here as those who have joyfully celebrated the
best of all birthdays.

ALL: **We rejoice that we are members of the Jesus family.**
We celebrate in the good times and care in the tough
times.
We meet around God's Word for guidance, and praise
wholeheartedly.
We are the weak who need support and the strong who
can give support.
We are those in the neighbourhood who need a home
and those overseas who are seeking a homeland.

ONE: Young and old, rich and poor, healthy and suffering,
gay and straight, from the bottom of our hearts *we*
shout,

ALL: **Happy birthday church! Happy birthday church!**

Trinity Sunday

1st Sunday after Pentecost

Proverbs 8:1–4, 22–31
Psalm 8
Romans 5:1–5
John 16:12–15

God's love has been poured into our hearts

ONE: Wonderful God, Creator, and natural leader of all humanity,

ALL: you welcome us to worship.

ONE: Jesus the Christ, chosen one of God, pattern of compassion and light in the darkness,

ALL: you welcome us to worship.

ONE: Holy Spirit, gift at Pentecost, inspiration without end, and partner in all our faithful endeavours,

ALL: you welcome us to worship, and we will worship joyfully.

Opening Prayer

ONE: Holy Spirit, truth bringer, you are with us.

ALL: God's love will bind us together in this faith community.

ONE: Holy Spirit, truth bringer, you are with us.

ALL: God's love will enable us to see the dark places, and to change them through the light of Christ.

ONE: Holy Spirit, truth bringer, you are with us.

ALL: God's love will expose the depth of our fear, and free us from its power.

ONE: Holy Spirit, truth bringer, you are with us.

ALL: God's love will confront the areas of injustice, and give us strength to bring change. Amen.

A Prayer Reflecting on God's Greatness
(from Psalm 8)

ONE: You call us, glorious God, to look up at the sky and to remember the limitless extent of your creation.

ALL: **We will look up and consider our crucial need to keep creation good.**

ONE: You call us, friendly God, to look around at the diversity of our fellow men and women, girls and boys.

ALL: **We will find ways to compassionately care for the challenged, the sick, and the vulnerable.**

ONE: You call us, wonderful God, to recognize the talents of those we know well and those who work and play with us.

ALL: **We will support those who try out new skills and set out on new ventures.**

ONE: You call us, eternal God, to acknowledge your timeless responsibility for humankind,

ALL: **We will praise your greatness, your supremacy in time and beyond time.** *(time of silent reflection)*

Assurance of God's Continuing Care

ONE: In moments of joy and at the time of thanksgiving,

ALL: **God is gloriously with us.**

ONE: At times when we could care less, at times when we avoid the Holy One,

ALL: **God is waiting for us.**

ONE: When we are downhearted, when life deals us hard blows,

ALL: **God will never leave us.**

ONE: We may neglect God, we may forget God,

ALL: **but God knows our name, God cares what happens to us, we have an Eternal Friend.**
Thanks be to you, our God. Amen.

Offering Prayer

ONE: Praise God, the source of life, the giver of all good gifts.

ALL: **Remember Jesus whose life story brings us together and calls us to serve with care and generosity.**

ONE: Work with the Holy Spirit,

ALL: **who inspires us to confront evil and to stand with the downtrodden. Amen.**

 Pastoral Prayer Pattern *(Romans 5:1–5)*

ONE: Love comes through the Holy Spirit

ALL: **and what seemed impossible now becomes possible. We can help love along. We can help**

ONE: women without affordable daycare find it.

children struggling in the school system get teacher assistance.

workers made redundant by robots be introduced to new areas of working.

unskilled, labouring people find trade training programs... *(current example)*

refugees settle into a permanent home... *(current example)*

prisoners receive the mental health care they need... *(current example)*

Love comes through the Holy Spirit

ALL: **and what seemed impossible now becomes possible. We can help love along.**

ONE: Love comes through the Holy Spirit,

ALL: **and what seemed impossible now becomes possible. We can help love along.**

ONE: The Good News is proclaimed with help from contemporary technology.

The needs of children/the housebound are given a first priority in the faith community.

Giving to the mission fund is valued as much as giving
to the local church.
Neighborhood needs are sought out and met.
Love comes through the Holy Spirit

ALL: **and what seemed impossible now becomes possible.
We can help love along.**

Commissioning

ONE: You are the change-makers of the Holy One;

ALL: **life will be different and good.**

ONE: You are the peacemakers of the Holy One;

ALL: **conflict and disharmony will be resolved.**

ONE: You are the health-bringers of the Holy One;

ALL: **suffering and sadness will be overcome.
The Love of God will enfold us, the example of Jesus
will enthuse us, the Holy Spirit will go with us. Amen.**

Sunday between June 12 and 18 inclusive

Proper 6 [11]

1 Kings 21:1–10, (11–14), 15–21a
Psalm 5:1–8
Galatians 2:15–21
Luke 7:36 – 8:3

Jesus is given a gift by a generous and loving woman

Call to Worship *(Psalm 5:7)*

ONE: Why do we come to worship?
ALL: **God's great love has called us here.**
ONE: A love to challenge us,
ALL: **a love to reassure us,**
ONE: a love to strengthen us,
ALL: **a love to work with us,**
ONE: a love to inspire us,
ALL: **a compassionate love.**
ONE: We have come to worship.
ALL: **God's Love will encounter us here.**

Opening Prayer

ONE: Generosity is your way, loving God.
ALL: **We will bring you wholehearted prayer and praise.**
ONE: Generosity is your way, loving God.
ALL: **We will share our gifts freely in this faith community.**
ONE: Generosity is your way, loving God.
ALL: **We will search out the downtrodden and help them.**
ONE: Generosity is your way, loving God.
ALL: **We will rejoice in the pattern of generosity Jesus
showed us and follow him. Amen.**

A Prayer of Forgiveness

ONE: Loving God, you call us to go the extra mile when it comes to forgiveness, but we find it hard to forgive with generosity.

ALL: **We find it difficult to forgive the family member or friend who has hurt us without cause.** *(time of silent reflection)*

ONE: You will forgive and make clear your will to begin again.

ALL: **We find it difficult to forgive those people who have held a grudge against us for a long time.** *(time of silent reflection)*

ONE: You will forgive with words of reconciliation.

ALL: **We find it difficult to forgive those in the church whose practice or vision run counter to ours.** *(time of silent reflection)*

ONE: You will forgive with listening and dialogue.

ALL: **We find it difficult to forgive the politicians and leaders whose policies and actions cause harm to the vulnerable and to children.** *(time of silent reflection)*

ONE: You will forgive with words of protest and active compassion.

ALL: **We will forgive. We will go the extra mile.**

Assurance of Forgiveness

ONE: We do not have the strength to change our words and actions, generous Spirit, loving God.

ALL: **You will encourage us; you will inspire us to effect the change we want so passionately to happen.**

ONE: On your own you may not be able to accomplish your goals,

ALL: **but working with the Holy Spirit there is nothing we cannot achieve.**
Thanks be to God. Amen.

Offering Prayer

ONE: We take time to count our blessings, Holy One.

ALL: **blessings of home and family, blessings of this church, blessings that arise because we are residents of this nation and inhabitants of the wonderful planet, Earth.** *(time of silent reflection)*

ONE: When we count our blessings, we find that they are grace-full and numberless,

ALL: **and we give thanks to you, Loving God, the creator and source of all that is good. Amen.**

 ### Pastoral Prayer Pattern *(from 1 Kings 21:1–10)*

ONE: We will make clear the abuse of power.

ALL: **We will work to bring change.**

ONE: We are aware of children labouring in unhealthy conditions in…*(current example).*

We are aware of older people who are afraid to speak up for themselves.

We are aware of those in our family circle and our faith community who are struggling to navigate the health system.

We are aware of those who are housebound or in hospital and are troubled. *(pray silently for them)*

We are aware of those who have lost loved ones and who cannot share their grief. *(we pray silently for them)*

We will make clear the abuse of power.

ALL: **We will work to bring change.**

ONE: We ourselves feel the abuse of the powerful.

ALL: **We will find the confidence to be changed.**

ONE: We will stand up to officials who will not listen to us.

We will stand up to family members or friends who try to manipulate us.

We will stand up to colleagues and group members who cause us to be what we are not.

We will stand up to those who persuade us to do what
we do not want to do.
We ourselves feel the abuse of the powerful.

ALL: **We will find the confidence to be changed.**

Commissioning

ONE: Servants of Jesus Christ, you have been called to
action.

ALL: **God's call is to give generously.**
God's call is to receive thankfully.
God's call is to welcome openly.
God's call is to share big-heartedly.
God's call is to be up front about our apathy.
God's call is to fight injustice persistently.
God's call is to identify with the vulnerable.

ONE: Servants of Jesus Christ, through action you will bring
change,

ALL: **and through change we will honour the name of Jesus.**

Sunday between June 19 and 25 inclusive

Proper 7 [12]

1 Kings 19:1–15a
Psalm 42 and 43
Galatians 3:23–29
Luke 8:26–39

The man possessed by demons is cured

Call to Worship *(from 1 Kings 19:12)*

ONE: We come, loving God, to hear your soft whisper of a voice.

ALL: **We will listen carefully.**

ONE: We come with our faith community friends.

ALL: **We will listen together.**

ONE: We come from different places and circumstances.

ALL: **We will listen with empathy.**

ONE: We come realizing the challenges that lie before us.

ALL: **We will listen and be strengthened.**

ONE: We come to hear your soft whisper of a voice in worship

ALL: **and you will speak to us beyond this worship time and place, and we give thanks, Loving God.**

Opening Prayer *(Psalm 42)*

ONE: As a parched person longs for a drink of cool water, so we long for you, Holy One.

ALL: **Sometimes we feel you have let us down, deserted us.**

ONE: We look back to large congregations and vibrant Sunday schools,

ALL: **when churches were attracting many new members, and the sanctuary was the place to be on Sunday morning.**

ALL: **We wonder, what went wrong?**

ONE: We feel profoundly sad that shopping, outings, and sports have replaced the worship of you, our loving God.

ALL: **We believe that your love will win through. We believe that your vital compassion will be a beacon to our troubled world.**

ONE: So, we will not stay downhearted, we will not be depressed by those who have forgotten your just and faithful ways.

ALL: **We hope for better days, Holy One. We will work to bring closer the time when your glorious presence is known and acknowledged all over the world. Amen.**

A Prayer for Healing

ONE: When we need to be healed, you are the source, O God.

ALL: **You meet us in the darkest place; in the place where we feel you to be absent, you are present.**

ONE: When we need to be healed, you are the source, O God.

ALL: **You meet us when we are tested and tried, and when we are ready to give up you bring us hope.**

ONE: When we need to be healed, you are the source, O God.

ALL: **You meet us when our sickness cannot be seen, and with good hands and minds you renew us.**

ONE: When we need to be healed, you are the source, O God.

ALL: **You meet us when our spirits are at the lowest point, and through prayer and meditation you make us whole again.** *(time of silent reflection)*

Assurance of Support

ONE: The ministry of healing is our ministry, compassionate God.

ALL: **Where diagnosis is difficult, we will be a patient presence.**

ONE: The ministry of healing is our ministry, compassionate God.

ALL: **Where treatment is long and slow, we will gently encourage.**

ONE: The ministry of healing is our ministry, compassionate God.

ALL: **Where home life is disrupted, we will find ways to lend a hand.**

ONE: The ministry of healing is our ministry, compassionate God.

ALL: **In the face of dying, and when life comes to an end, we will enable the grief that gently restores the living. Amen.**

Offering Prayer

ONE: Good gifts, loving God, make possible the sharing of Good News.

ALL: **We will not keep the compassion of Jesus to ourselves.**

ONE: Within our faith community,

ALL: **we will teach young and old alike the stories of Jesus, and we will equip them to work the Jesus way.**

ONE: Outside our faith community and through the mission fund,

ALL: **we will support those who are voiceless and downtrodden, and with practical help and money bring hope. Amen.**

Pastoral Prayer Pattern

ONE: We know what Good News stories would be,

ALL: **but we cannot yet tell the Good News:**

ONE: that greenhouse gasses have been reduced and the oceans cleaned up,

that all refugees in Jordan and Southern Sudan have a
new homeland,
that women and girls are no longer at risk,
that rich nations will no longer exploit the resources of
developing nations.
As we wait to tell the Good News,
we will pray and work and advocate for change.

ONE: We know what Good News stories would be,
ALL: **but we cannot yet tell the Good News:**
ONE: that all major denominations welcome each other's
members to the Holy Communion table,
that the most vulnerable in our area are given food
and shelter by a common group of churches,
that a joint ministry of nursing and healing is practiced
in our local area,
that the national leaders of faith groups will jointly
speak out for protecting the environment and for the
most vulnerable.
As we wait to tell the good news,
ALL: **we will pray and work and advocate for change.**

Commissioning

ONE: Heal through words and actions.
ALL: **We will heal and we will challenge where there is
oppression and distrust.**
ONE: Heal through words and actions.
ALL: **We will heal and we will give confidence to those who
are afraid.**
ONE: Heal through words and actions.
ALL: **We will heal, and we will not forget the youngest and
most vulnerable.**
ONE: You will heal through words and actions, and by this
you will show your faithfulness to Jesus the Christ.

Sunday between June 26 and July 2 inclusive

Proper 8 [13]

2 Kings 2:1–2, 6–14
Psalm 77:1–2, 11–20
Galatians 5:1, 13–25
Luke 9:51–62

Jesus makes up his mind to go to Jerusalem

Call to Worship (*from 2 Kings 2:9*)

ONE: Come to share the spirit of the prophets.

ALL: We will come close to God, as they did.

ONE: Come to share the fearlessness of the prophets.

ALL: We will confront the powerful ones of our time.

ONE: Come to share the justice-bringing work of the prophets.

ALL: We will speak and act for the poor and downtrodden.

ONE: Come to share the commitment of the prophets.

ALL: We will work unsparingly for our loving God.

Opening Prayer of Determination (*from Luke 9:51*)

ONE: We seek the determination of Jesus, who made up his mind to go to Jerusalem.

ALL: We will keep our eyes on the most faithful goal.

ONE: There are those who will seek to discourage us.

ALL: We will listen but we will not look back.

ONE: There are those who are not open to our mission.

ALL: We will encounter them but keep our vision bright.

ONE: There are those who will oppose us.

ALL: **We will dialogue with them and make clear why we have chosen to go forward.**

ONE: Your faithful determination will carry you through.

ALL: **Thanks be to God. Amen.**

A Prayer of Discipleship

ONE: We give thanks that we can follow Jesus with all the joy and responsibility that comes with that choice.

ALL: **We will follow Jesus and rejoice in the friends we make,**

ONE: and we will be ready for indifference, ready to accept rejection.

ALL: **We will follow Jesus and rejoice in the opportunities that open up,**

ONE: and we will be ready for opposition, ready for the hard work.

ALL: **We will follow Jesus when life is going well for us,**

ONE: and we will be prepared for the times when life is difficult and challenging.

ALL: **We will follow Jesus when we are young and passionate,**

ONE: and will be prepared for the infirmity and uncertainty of old age.

ALL: **We will follow Jesus when we are able to support and commend our leaders,**

ONE: and we will be prepared to oppose those who lack compassion and a sense of what is just. *(time of silent reflection)*

Assurance of Peace along the Way

ONE: We pray for peace, Loving God.
       When the community of faith is weak,

ALL: **peace in prayer, praise, and holy silence.**

ONE: When the community of faith is strong,

ALL: **peace in caring for the vulnerable and in helping those who are drifting.**

ONE: When we are downhearted,

ALL: **peace from the presence of loved ones.**

ONE: When we are on top of the world,

ALL: **peace as we share our joy with others. Amen.**

Offering Prayer

ONE: Our gifts are given to support this faith community in good times and hard times.

ALL: **We ask you to bless them, loving God.**

ONE: Our gifts are given to support the mission work of our denomination: healing work, confidence-bringing work.

ALL: **We ask you to bless them, loving God.**

ONE: Our gifts are given to support so many faithful people, in this place and overseas.

ALL: **We ask you to bless them, loving God. Amen.**

💔 Pastoral Prayer Pattern

ONE: We are aware of those who are challenged.

ALL: **We are committed to serve.**

ONE: Job searchers who are finding new opportunities hard to come by need our support.
Young adults struggling to overcome peer pressure to drink and experiment with addictive drugs need our support.
Sufferers from cancer whose treatment is delayed need our support.
Friends and family as well as church family friends who are ill in hospital and at home need our presence and prayers *(time of silent reflection)*
Friends who have lost loved ones need our comfort and care. *(time of silent reflection)*
We are aware of those who are challenged, but

ALL: **we are committed to serve.**

ONE: We are aware of our own challenges, but

ALL: we are committed to serve.

ONE: We have found reasons not to give our faith high priority, but will make changes.

We have been reluctant to care for the downtrodden and despised, but will seek them out.

We have been aware of hidden conflicts within the family circle, and will face these conflicts.

We have determined our life goals, and now will work to achieve them.

We are aware of our own challenges, but

ALL: we are committed to serve.

Commissioning

ONE: With minds made up, we leave this church.

ALL: We will pray faithfully.

We will proclaim the Good News joyfully.

We will advance the Jesus-way appropriately.

We will banish apathy thoroughly.

ONE: With minds made up we leave this church

ALL: to bring peace to the suffering,

to give comfort to the grieving,

to bring hope to the despairing,

and to bring love to those who feel unloved.

ONE: God goes with us on our journey.

Sunday between July 3rd and 9th

Proper 9 [14]

2 Kings 5:1–14
Psalm 30
Galatians 6:(1–6), 7–16
Luke 10:1–11, 16–20

Jesus sends out 72 disciples

Call to Worship

ONE: We come to share our joy in Christ:

ALL: **Christ's words, Christ's work, Christ's faithfulness to God.**

ONE: We come to share our love in Christian community:

ALL: **a love to ease the hurts, a love to end conflicts, a love to forge a vision.**

ONE: We come to share our hope of peace:

ALL: **peace for those we love, peace within the faith community, peace in our neighbourhood, peace for our troubled world.**

ONE: We come, ready to share our sense of justice:

ALL: **justice for those denied freedom, justice for women and children, justice for those persecuted for political action.**
We come as those prepared for discipleship.

Opening Prayer of Thanks *(from Psalm 30:6–12)*

ONE: Remember what the Holy One has done and give God thanks.

ALL: **God is good; we have seen that goodness in our wonderful creation.**

ONE: Give God thanks.

ALL: **God is to be trusted; our security lies with God.**

ONE: Give God thanks.

ALL: **God is merciful; we are given the chance to begin again.**

ONE: Give God thanks.

ALL: **God meets us when we have suffered loss and will not leave us without hope.**

ONE: Give God thanks.

ALL: **God's ever-present love goes beyond time and space. Amen.**

A Prayer of Preparation for Jesus *(from Luke 10:1)*

ONE: We are sent ahead to show clearly the way of Jesus Christ.

ALL: **Despite the indifference, despite the opposition, we will persevere.**

ONE: We are sent ahead and the work is not easy.

ALL: **We will trust in our abilities. We will go forward with urgency.**

ONE: We are sent ahead as peace-bringers.

ALL: **Whether we are received with joy, or just tolerated, we will work to bring peace.**

ONE: We are sent ahead and are grateful for hospitality.

ALL: **We will respect our hosts and seek to help and to heal.**

ONE: We are sent ahead to highlight the needs of the downtrodden.

ALL: **We will stand with them and confront the powerful.**

ONE: This is the way that God's realm comes closer.

ALL: **We are about the work of Jesus the Christ.** *(time of silent reflection)*

Assurance of Faithfulness

ONE: As followers of Jesus, we are called to be faithful.

ALL: **The words of Jesus inspire us.**
        The stories of Jesus have meaning for us.
        The courage of Jesus motivates us.

> The stand of Jesus against evil is clear for us.
> The powerful leaders ranged against Jesus humble us.
> We ask the question: "As present-day disciples, can we follow faithfully?"

ONE: With God nothing is impossible. Trust God and Christ's way for you will come clear.

ALL: **Amen.**

Offering Prayer (*from Galatians 6:2*)

ONE: Enable us, loving God, through these gifts to bear each other's burdens:

ALL: **to support the lonely and downhearted,**
to stand with the bereaved,
to bring Christian teaching to young and old alike,
to train for leadership and care for our leaders,
to help through the mission fund those whose names we will never know.

ONE: In this way, you will obey the law of Christ.

ALL: **Thanks be to God. Amen.**

🌐 Pastoral Prayer Pattern

ONE: God calls you to practical but faithful tasks.

ALL: **We will respond as we are able.**

ONE: Some political prisoners are without legal rights.

ALL: **We will write for their release.**

ONE: Refugees still stream over the borders of hostile nations.

ALL: **We will give to refugee groups. We will consider hosting refugees in our own community.**

ONE: Some political leaders treat climate change with complacency.

ALL: **We will confront them with the need for urgent action.**

ONE: Some retired people cannot find practical ways of using their time.

ALL: **We will take time to direct them to volunteer opportunities.**

ONE: God calls you to practical but faithful tasks.

ALL: **We will respond as we are able.**

ONE: God calls you to practical but faithful tasks.

ALL: **We will respond as we are able.**

ONE: There are opportunities to grow spiritually as followers of Jesus Christ,

ALL: **We will search out resources and leaders and give time to prayer and meditation.**

ONE: There are opportunities to teach, to care, and to serve in the local faith community.

ALL: **We will review our skills and offer to help.**

ONE: There are opportunities to serve with local people who need friends, advocates, and mentors *(local examples).*

ALL: **We will explore the possibilities to help and get involved.**

ONE: God calls you to practical but faithful tasks.

ALL: **We will respond as we are able.**

Commissioning

ONE: There is a harvest to be gathered for the Christian cause. You are challenged to be among those who gather the harvest.

ALL: **As harvesters, we will know when to speak and when to listen.**
We will know those to approach and those to avoid.
We will know the times of opportunity and the inopportune times.
We will know the scriptures that are appropriate and those that are not helpful.
We will be ready to work practically and pray carefully.

ONE: Remember the words of Jesus: "There is a large harvest but few workers to gather it in."

Sunday between July 10 and 16 inclusive

Proper 10 [15]

Amos 7:7–17
Psalm 82
Colossians 1:1–14
Luke 10:25–37

The parable of the Good Samaritan

Call to Worship

ONE: This is a good place to be.

ALL: **In our readings, the prophet speaks of faithfulness.**

ONE: This is a good place to be.

ALL: **In our readings, the psalmist speaks of justice.**

ONE: This is a good place to be.

ALL: **In our readings, the letter writer speaks of giving thanks with joy.**

ONE: This is a good place to be.

ALL: **In our readings, the evangelist speaks of loving your neighbour.**

ONE: This is a good place to be.

ALL: **We are glad we are here.**

Opening Prayer

ONE: We worship God, who calls us to compassion.

ALL: **We will be looking out for the needs around us.**

ONE: We worship God, who calls us to compassion.

ALL: **We will give practical help to the troubled.**

ONE: We worship God, who calls us to compassion.

ALL: **We will be there for the duration of need.**

ONE: We worship God, who calls us to compassion.

ALL: **We will cultivate a pattern of support and help.**

ONE: Thanks be to God.

ALL: **Amen.**

Prayer of Ministering to Our Neighbour

ONE: Loving God, when our neighbour is in distress,

ALL: **we are called to a ministry of listening.**

ONE: When our neighbour has practical needs or wants,

ALL: **we are called to a ministry of assistance.**

ONE: When our neighbour faces discrimination,

ALL: **we are called to a ministry of inclusion and support.**

ONE: When our overseas neighbour is without necessary supplies or confidence,

ALL: **we are called to a ministry of sharing and assurance.**

The Assurance of Being a Good Neighbour.

ONE: When pressure at home or at work weighs neighbours down,

ALL: **we will support and assist them.**

ONE: When we are going through hard times,

ALL: **we will graciously accept the help of our neighbour.**

ONE: When there is a common neighourhood need,

ALL: **we will willingly share in meeting that need.**

ONE: When we encounter people who are despised or challenged,

ALL: **we will identify them as "our neighbours."**

ONE: Good neighbours help others find fulfillment and peace.

ALL: **It is, thanks be to God. Amen.**

Offering Prayer

ONE: These gifts will sustain our neighbours in Jesus Christ.

ALL: **Those with ministry roles will find encouragement. Those with leadership responsibilities will sense our backing.**

The housebound will be visited and the sick remembered.
Children and youth will grow in the faith.
Members of other faith groups will be welcomed and the wider church will know our thanks and support.

ONE: We will not take these gifts for granted
ALL: **and God will bless them as they go to work. Amen.**

 Pastoral Prayer Pattern

ONE: "I am your neighbour."
ALL: **The words take us by surprise.**
ONE: Before us we see a faithful church member who cannot leave her home.
ALL: **"I am your neighbour."**
ONE: Before us we see sick family members and church family members who would appreciate a visit.
ALL: **"I am your neighbour."**
ONE: Before us we see we see friends who have suffered loss and who need our support.
ALL: **"I am your neighbour."**
ONE: Before us we see children coming back to an empty home after school who may need a refuge in time of trouble.
"I am your neighbour."
ALL: **The words take us by surprise.**

ONE: "I am your neighbour."
ALL: **The words take us by surprise.**
ONE: In our mind's eye we see an abused refugee woman in Lebanon searching for a ray of hope.
ALL: **"I am your neighbour."**
ONE: In our mind's eye we see a person near to us who needs to forgive or to be forgiven.
ALL: **"I am your neighbour."**

ONE: In our mind's eye we see a friend who believes that we will be able to live our most cherished dream.

ALL: **"I am your neighbour."**

ONE: In our mind's eye we see a family member who has suffered loss and who needs our help. *(time of silent reflection)*

"I am your neighbour."

ALL: **The words take us by surprise.**

Commissioning

ONE: As we leave this church, living God, we wonder, "Who is our neighbour?"

ALL: **It is a good question, enabling us to think about our answer.**

"Who is our neighbour?" *(time of silent reflection)*

ONE: Give us fresh resolution to help our neighbours and the determination to work with them for the common good. *(time of silent reflection)*

ALL: **Broaden our understanding of the term "neighbour."**

We have neighbours next door and upstairs, but we also have neighbours in the workplace and in our social groups.

We have neighbours who live close by and those who are half a world away.

We have neighbours of our culture and those who think and act and feel very differently from the way we do. *(time of silent reflection)*

How can we help them? How can they be invited to help us? *(time of silent reflection)*

ONE: Go from this church resolved to be a good neighbour, a "Good Samaritan."

or

ONE: Go from the church to be "Good Samaritans."

ALL: **We will be there for our family and friends when trouble comes.**

We will be there for our fellow church members in their tough times.
We will go out of our way to help the person who is despised and abused.
We will sustain our assistance and advocate for change.
We will gracefully accept help when we need help.

ONE: In your giving, in your receiving, you will be richly blessed.

Sunday between July 17 and 23 inclusive

Proper 11[16]

Amos 8:1–12
Psalm 52
Colossians 1:15–28
Luke 10:38–42

Jesus visits Martha and Mary

Call to Worship *(from Psalm 52)*

ONE: God can always be trusted.

ALL: We come joyfully to worship God.

ONE: God's justice is clear and understandable.

ALL: We will treat people fairly.

ONE: God's love calls us to care.

ALL: We will practice compassion.

ONE: God's love is without limits of time and space.

ALL: We will thank God eternally.

Opening Prayer *(from Colossians 1:23)*

ONE: Your foundation is Jesus Christ.

ALL: We will listen to his teaching carefully.

ONE: Your foundation is Jesus Christ.

ALL: We will work in his way enthusiastically.

ONE: Your foundation is Jesus Christ.

ALL: We will join with other Christians joyfully.

ONE: Your foundation is Jesus Christ.

ALL: We have a gospel hope that is unshakeable, a gospel hope that goes beyond all limits. Amen.

A Prayer of Diverse Gifts *(from Luke 10:18–42)*

The congregation may be divided into two sections for this prayer: right side (RS) and left side (LS).

ONE: Creator God, you have given each one of us a variety of gifts, and we thank you.

RS: Some of us have the gift of practical hospitality.

LS: Some of us have the gift of spiritual curiosity.

ONE: You have gifts to practically help others and gifts to satisfy your souls.

RS: Some of us have the gift of prayer.

LS: Some of us have the gift of singing hymns and songs.

ONE: With those gifts you can faithfully worship God.

RS: Some of us have the gifts of leadership and organization.

LS: Some of us have the gift of scriptural reflection and preaching.

ONE: You have gifts to strengthen the faith community.

RS: Some of us have the gift of teaching,

LS: Some of us have the gift of visiting the sick.

ONE: You have inspiring and compassionate gifts.

RS: We are happy to share our gifts in this faith community.

LS: We are happy to receive the gifts of others. *(time of silent reflection)*

ONE: You have received your gifts from God, and it is to the glory of God that you use them.

An Assurance that All Good Gifts Can Be Used

ONE: Loving God, you call us to name and identify our gifts and abilities.

ALL: **You challenge us to search out our own unused gifts and to use them.**
You call us to point out and put to use the unrecognized gifts of others.
Where we are uncertain about using our gifts, loving God, give us the courage to get started.

Where we can see fresh gifts in others and they resist,
give us patient persistence.
Where we lack self-confidence to use our gifts,
encourage us, loving God.
Where others lack self-confidence, may we be the ones
who gently encourage them.

ONE: Pray that the graceful gifts we have received will go to
work for God, and know that God forgives us when we
fall short of using our gifts to the full. Amen.

Offering Prayer

ONE: We give these gifts so that God's work can be done:

ALL: **the practical work of providing food for the hungry,
the compassionate work of staying beside the sick and
the bereaved,
the spiritual work of opening the scriptures and of
explaining their significance for today.**

ONE: Bless these gifts, O God, as they are used in our
church. And bless the gifts that bring hope and
fulfilment through our mission fund.

ALL: **Amen.**

Pastoral Prayer Pattern

ONE: There are practical needs and there are thought-full
needs.

ALL: **We will respond compassionately.**

ONE: The frail elderly and the very young will know our
caring.
The pain-burdened will experience our
encouragement.
The anxious and depressed will be able to talk out
their feelings with us.
Those suddenly sick will be able to count on us to
support their families.
We reflect on those we know who are going through
hard times. *(time of silent reflection)*

We will help practically the bereaved, and we will be a gentle presence to them. *(time of silent reflection)*
There are practical needs and there are thought-full needs.

ALL: **We will respond compassionately.**

ONE: There are practical needs and there are thought-full needs.

ALL: **We will respond compassionately.**

ONE: There is coffee to make and there are sandwiches and cake to supply for meetings.
There are faith groups to lead and there is prayer to be offered.
There are rides to give to the hospital and there are prescriptions to fetch from the drug store.
There are other churches and other faith groups with which to share worship and discussion.
There are practical needs and there are thought-full needs.

ALL: **We will respond compassionately.**

Commissioning

ONE: You are a wonderfully gifted people. Put your gifts to work in the service of Jesus Christ.

ALL: **We will give gifts of resourcefulness to help save our planet.**
We will give gifts of care-full-ness to bring hope to the suffering.
We will give teaching gifts and the gift of befriending to inspire children and youth.
We will employ gifts of leadership to nurture this faith community.
We will advocate and challenge to help refugees and forgotten political prisoners.

ONE: With your commitment, there is nothing we cannot achieve. The name of Jesus will be honoured by your giving.

ALL: **We give humbly. We give joyfully. Amen.**

Sunday between July 24 and 30 inclusive

Proper 12 [17]

Hosea 1:2–10
Psalm 85
Colossians 2:6–15, (16–19)
Luke 11:1–13

The Lord's Prayer...perseverance in prayer

Call to Worship

ONE: This is the place to be on Sunday morning.

ALL: **We rejoice in our time of worship.**

ONE: These are the people to be with on Sunday morning:

ALL: **our friends and fellow church members.**

ONE: These are the words of life, the words in scripture:

ALL: **words that are full of truth and challenge, words that inspire.**

ONE: These are the prayers offered in faith community:

ALL: **the Lord's Prayer, listening prayers, prayers that stir us to action.**

ONE: This is the gift we receive as followers of Jesus Christ:

ALL: **the Good News for our world, our church, and ourselves today; the Good News that will transform the coming days.**

Opening Prayer

ONE: We are with you in prayer, loving God.

ALL: **We praise you; we honour your name.**

ONE: We are with you in prayer, loving God.

ALL: **We will work to bring closer your realm of justice and peace.**

ONE: You are with us in prayer, loving God.

ALL: **We thank you for the food we have day by day, and we will work so that the hungry will be fed.**

ONE: You are with us in prayer, loving God.

ALL: **We will forgive friends and enemies and accept the forgiveness of others.**

ONE: You are with us in prayer, loving God.

ALL: **And in all the challenges that come in this life, we know that you will stay with us. Amen.**

A Prayer of Persistence *(from Luke 11:5–14)*

ONE: When our spiritual life feels dead, when prayer seems like speaking to ourselves,

ALL: **Loving Spirit, you call us to persevere.**

ONE: When our efforts to help and care go without response, when our compassion meets with rejection,

ALL: **Loving Spirit, you call us to persevere.**

ONE: When our concerns for the faith community are disregarded, when the talents we offer are not used,

ALL: **Loving Spirit, you call us to persevere.**

ONE: When our concerns for the neighbourhood are not shared, when our enthusiasm for an overseas project is ignored,

ALL: **Loving Spirit, you call us to persevere.** *(time of silent reflection)*

Assurance of Action

ONE: You are the counterpoint to apathy and inaction, loving Spirit.

ALL: **Where the spiritual is ignored, you bring prayer and contemplation.**
Where compassion is unwelcome, you bring warmth and understanding.
Where there are hard feelings in the faith community, you bring peace and a willingness to work things out.

> **Where there is a reluctance to get involved in reform or political action, you bring a sense of justice without borders.**

ONE: Loving Spirit, as we become a positive Christian presence,

ALL: **so you will strengthen and encourage us, and we will find joy in our calling to serve you. Amen.**

Offering Prayer

ONE: Children of the living God, with your gifts come responsibility.

ALL: **We will compassionately care for the downhearted and sick of our faith community.**
We will join with other faiths to share stories and to work for peace.
We will be alert to the needs of our neighbourhood.
We will give generously for the exploited beyond our shores through the *mission fund*.

ONE: With your caring, in your sharing with others, in your zeal for justice and peace, your gifts will be blessed.

ALL: **Thanks be to God. Amen.**

 ### Pastoral Prayer Pattern

ONE: Generous and far-seeing God,

ALL: **you call us to go the extra mile:**

ONE: not just to give money to help refugees, but to care for refugee families;
not just to write letters to help political prisoners, but to speak of their plight at embassies and consulates;
not just to write or march in protest against climate change deniers, but to share our views with political representatives;
not just to write letters about pressing local issues, but to attend appropriate meetings.
Generous and far-seeing God,

ALL: **you call us to go the extra mile.**

ONE: Generous and far-seeing God,

ALL: **you call us to go the extra mile.**

ONE: We will go out of our way to help a family member or a friend.
We will find a practical or personal way to help someone who has suffered a significant loss.
We will work out a way to help a sick person keep their pet.
We will be prepared to endure hardship if it means that a young person will find heath or a positive way.
Generous and far-seeing God,

ALL: **you call us to go the extra mile.**

Commissioning

ONE: Pray without ceasing and act on what you pray.

ALL: **We will pray for those in our world who need God's compassion.** *(time of silent reflection)*

ONE: Pray without ceasing.

ALL: **We will pray for family members and for friends who are going through tough times.** *(time of silent reflection)*

ONE: Pray without ceasing.

ALL: **We will pray for our faith community and for those who need our support.** *(time of silent reflection)*

ONE: Pray without ceasing.

ALL: **We will pray for ourselves that we will have the courage to use our talents.** *(time of silent reflection)*

ONE: Pray without ceasing, and act on what you pray.

Sunday between July 31 and August 6 inclusive

Proper 13 [18]

Hosea 11:1–11
Psalm 107:1–9, 43
Colossians 3:1–11
Luke 12:13–21

How to be rich in God's sight

Call to Worship *(from Psalm 107:43)*

ONE: God's love is with this faith community,

ALL: and we rejoice in God's constant love.

ONE: In this service of worship, we sing and pray to God,

ALL: and we rejoice in God's constant love.

ONE: We are guided through Hebrew and Christian scriptures,

ALL: and we rejoice in God's constant love.

ONE: We proclaim the Good News of Jesus Christ,

ALL: and we rejoice in God's constant love.

ONE: We will go out to serve, and as we serve,

ALL: we will rejoice in God's constant love.

Opening Prayer *(from Hosea 11:1–11)*

ONE: You are God's children; you have nothing to fear.

ALL: Like children, we stray from the right way, but God corrects us.

ONE: You are God's children.

ALL: Like children, we disobey, but God forgives us.

ONE: You are God's children.

ALL: Like children, we are sure that we know best, but God still loves us.

ONE: You are God's children.

ALL: **Like children, we ignore the wisdom of our Loving Parent, but God will enlighten us.
We are God's children, and we have nothing to fear.
Amen.**

A Prayer of Searching for the True Life

ONE: We search for the true life, the life that deeply satisfies. We search for this life by acquiring wealth and possessions,

ALL: **but the true life cannot be bought and sold.**

ONE: We search for the true life by going to social events,

ALL: **but the true life is not found at parties.**

ONE: We search for the true life in a bigger house, a lavish holiday,

ALL: **but the true life is not to be had on cruises or in real estate.**

ONE: We search for the true life as we eat well and drink well,

ALL: **but the true life is not found in big meals or at fancy restaurants.**

ONE: "You can't take your wealth with you," says Jesus.

ALL: **How right he is. How right he is.** *(time of silent reflection)*

A Prayer of Finding the Life that Satisfies

ONE: In a growing relationship with a child or grandchild,

ALL: **true life is sensed.**

ONE: In a job that satisfies or a vocation that deeply fulfills,

ALL: **true life comes clear.**

ONE: In a volunteer task of compassion, a skill used to help a neighbour,

ALL: **true life is discovered.**

ONE: In a prayer or meditation time that calms, a book that inspires fresh insights,

ALL: **true life is revealed.**

ONE: Give thanks to God for the aspects of true life that are yours.

ALL: **We thank God, who is the source of all in our life that is good and true. Amen.**

Offering Prayer

ONE: You will bless, living God, money that is wisely and faithfully used.

ALL: **And so we bring these gifts for blessing.**
In our faith community, we will support one another.
In our faith community, we will find guidance in the scriptures.
In our faith community, we will stand with the sick and the bereaved.
In our faith community, we will offer praise and prayer.
From our faith community, we will go out to help the people of our neighbourhood.
From our faith community, we will give and speak out for the abandoned and the despised of our suffering world.

ONE: With your blessing, these gifts will go to work, living God.

ALL: **Your name will be honoured and the way of Jesus followed. Amen.**

 ### Pastoral Prayer Pattern

ONE: We seek to be rich in God's sight.

ALL: **The Jesus way shows us how.**

ONE: Those rich in God's sight search out the poor and give them confidence, hope, and a regular place for a square meal.
Those rich in God's sight are in tune with neighbourhood services that are lacking, and they advocate for those without adequate housing, and for those searching for work.

Those rich in God's sight cannot stand the sight of youngsters without adequate food or denied basic health services. They will advocate for them or help them with gifts.

Those rich in God's sight hate the subtle and not-so-subtle discrimination against women, and work to right this wrong.

We seek to be rich in God's sight,

ALL: **The Jesus way shows us how.**

ONE: We seek to be rich in God's sight.

ALL: **The Jesus way shows us how.**

ONE: Those rich in God's sight notice people whose talents and skills are ignored and encourage them to use those talents.

Those rich in God's sight are there for the downhearted, for people who are mentally sick, and for people with a physical disability. They are also aware of their own abilities and disabilities.

Those rich in God's sight support members of the faith community who are challenged by family or personal circumstances, and are a caring presence with them.

Those rich in God's sight are concerned for the sick, especially for those to whom illness has come unexpectedly. We pray silently for them. *(time of silent reflection)*

Those rich in God's sight are aware of those who have lost loved ones recently, and a while ago, and comfort them. We seek to be rich in God's sight.

ALL: **The Jesus way shows us how.**

Commissioning

ONE: Speak out for God's values in a money-driven world.

ALL: **We will call our friends and strangers to be still and resonate with God's creation beauty.**
We will call them to act compassionately where there is hurt, infirmity, and depression.
We will call them to speak out where there is poverty and a house that can never be a home.
We will call them to confront the power-hungry, the greedy, and the prejudiced.

ONE: God calls you to bring closer God's realm of justice and peace.

ALL: **This we will do, in the spirit of Jesus Christ.**

Sunday between August 7 and 13 inclusive

Proper 14 [19]

Isaiah 1:1, 10–20
Psalm 50:1–8, 22–23
Hebrews 11:1–3, 8–16
Luke 12:32–40

Be ready for whatever comes

Call to Worship *(from Isaiah 1:17)*

ONE: If it were just to praise and thank God,

ALL: **it would be good to be here.**

ONE: If it were just to meet and share news with members of this faith community,

ALL: **it would be good to be here.**

ONE: If it were just to pray for those who are sick and plan to visit those who can no longer come to church,

ALL: **it would be good to be here.**

ONE: But God has charged us with responsibility for our fellow human beings:

ONE: "See that justice is done, help those who are oppressed."

ALL: **God calls us to take our neighbourhood and global responsibilities seriously. It is good to be here.**

Opening Prayer *(from Hebrews 11:1–3,8–16)*

ONE: We are your people of faith, living God.

ALL: **We rejoice in your wonderful creation.**

ONE: We are your people of faith, living God.

ALL: **We have a basis for our faith in the Hebrew and Christian scriptures.**

ONE: We are your people of faith, living God.

ALL: **We are in the venturing tradition of Abraham and Sarah.**

ONE: We are your people of faith, living God.

ALL: **We will live faithfully in our day and generation.**

ONE: We are your people of faith, Living God.

ALL: **We look towards that day when your love will eternally embrace us. We will always be your people of faith. Amen.**

A Prayer of Being Prepared

ONE: Living God, you call us to be prepared. Are we ready? Ready to put what is past in the past?

ALL: **We are prepared to remember past setbacks, but move on.**

ONE: Are you ready? Ready to face the challenges of today?

ALL: **We are prepared to face the demands that test us directly.**

ONE: Are you ready? Ready to face the difficult encounters that lie ahead?

ALL: **We are prepared to face those with whom we do not see eye to eye with openness.**

ONE: Are you ready? Ready to face the unexpected twists and turns in life?

ALL: **We are prepared to face both joy and sorrow, with the strength that our Christian faith gives us.** *(time of silent reflection)*

Assurance of God's Help

ONE: It may seem you are on your own,

ALL: **but God's help is there for you.**

ONE: It may seem that your burden is too heavy to bear,

ALL: **but you will find those who will listen and those who will share the load.**

ONE: It may seem that there is no end to loss or suffering,

ALL: **but you *will* know an easier time, the faint glimmer of light in the dark.**

ONE: It may seem that friends and family members have deserted you,

ALL: **but you will know those who care, the surprising presence of compassionate ones.**

ONE: At the end of the day, peace will be yours –

ALL: **God's peace, which goes way beyond human understanding. Amen.**

Offering Prayer

ONE: You are ready to give money for the work of Jesus Christ, but are you ready to give more?

ALL: **We offer our time to build up this faith community, and to support its work.**
We offer our skills and talents to teach, to pray, to bring justice, and to care.

ONE: All your gifts are appreciated and will be blessed; the church will be blessed, the neighbourhood will be blessed, and through our mission fund, people world-wide will be blessed.

ALL: **Thanks, be to God. Amen.**

💔 Pastoral Prayer Pattern

ONE: We are called to be watchful.

ALL: **We will be ready to act.**

ONE: We will look out for the poor of this country and the starving overseas.
We will look out for church members who are in care homes and for all who are unable to attend worship.
We will look out for young people who keep to themselves, and for older people who cannot speak up for themselves.
We will look out for those of this faith community who are sick, and for those depressed, troubled, and in pain known only to us.

We offer them to you, in our heartfelt prayers,
compassionate God. *(time of silent reflection)*
We will look out for those who have been bereaved,
and for those who have suffered loss. *(time of silent
reflection)*
We are called to be watchful.

ALL: **We will be ready to act.**

ONE: We are called to be watchful.

ALL: **We will be ready to act.**

ONE: We will look out for those who come to our faith
community for the first time and welcome them with
sensitivity.
We will support those who lead and guide our faith
community, and give them a break when needed.
We will look out for opportunities to serve the
downtrodden and the despised of our local
community, and help them to find a good way forward.
We are called to be watchful.

ALL: **We will be ready to act.**

Commissioning

ONE: You are ready to go back to your small corner of this
wonderful world. Be on your toes.

ALL: **We are ready to help the very old and the very young,
and we are ready to receive the help that we are
offered.
We are ready to confront the powerful, call out the
evasive, and listen to the words that call us to reflect
and to question.
We are ready to speak of our Christian faith and we are
ready to listen to the truth that comes to us through
the Buddhist, Jewish, and Muslim faith traditions.**

ONE: Be ready for the unexpected. Be ready for a blessing.
Go in peace.

Sunday between August 14 and 20 inclusive

Proper 15 [20]

Isaiah 5:1–7
Psalm 80:1–2, 8–19
Hebrews 11:29 — 12:2
Luke 12:49–56

The faithful path will cause division

Call to Worship *(from Hebrews 12:2)*

ONE: Let us keep our eyes fixed on Jesus,

ALL: **who was faithful from beginning to end.**

ONE: Jesus called disciples from their regular work

ALL: **and was ready to bring hope to exploited people.**

ONE: Jesus met the downhearted and despised of his time

ALL: **and gave them a sense of their own self-worth.**

ONE: Jesus went out of his way for people who were mentally sick,

ALL: **and restored them to good health.**

ONE: Jesus confronted the power people of his time,

ALL: **and ended up dead, on a cross.**

ONE: If we keep our eyes fixed on Jesus, God's faithful one,

ALL: **life will be intensely good, but it will not be easy.**

Opening Prayer

ONE: You call us to choose, living God, and it is a hard choice.

ALL: **You call us to choose the faithful way or the easy way.**

ONE: You call us to choose, living God, and it is a hard choice.

ALL: **You call us to choose the well-trodden path or the way of adventure.**

ONE: You call us to choose, living God, and it is a hard choice.

ALL: **You call us to choose the comfortable life or the life of faithful uncertainty.**

ONE: You call us to choose, living God, and it is a hard choice.

ALL: **You call us to go with the crowd or to speak and act with integrity.**

ONE: It is hard to choose, but we follow Jesus, the one who made hard choices.

ALL: **In prayer and in practice, we will make clear our discipleship. Amen.**

A Prayer of Peace

ONE: It is not the peace of lasting calm and ease you promise us, living God,

ALL: **but the peace that comes from saying and doing what is right in your eyes, and not backing down.**

ONE: If a family is divided, and the just way prevails,

ALL: **if a faith community is at odds, but the truth is found and followed,**

ONE: if a social group cannot agree, but compromise is achieved,

ALL: **if a class has different viewpoints, and everyone has a say,**

ONE: it is your faithful peace we have been seeking, living God, the peace that lasts. *(time of silent reflection)*

Assurance of Peace in the Struggle

ONE: We will find the way to an authentic peace through the struggles of Jesus. The family of Jesus called on him to put them first on his list of priorities.
The way of peace?

ALL: **Jesus saw the health and faith needs of those around him and met those needs ahead of his family.**

ONE: The rulers and high priests called on him to go along
       with the accepted rules and traditions.
       The way of peace?

ALL: **Jesus saw the value of tradition but knew when to put it
       on one side.**

ONE: The powerful ones saw Jesus talking with prostitutes
       and with those who exploited the poor. They called
       him to account.
       The way of peace?

ALL: **Jesus saw the worth and potential of each person he
       encountered and was keen to develop that potential.**

ONE: The chief priests and Roman overlords saw Jesus as a
       threat to all that was important to them and their
       influential families.
       The ultimate way of peace?

ALL: **The cross. Amen.**

Offering Prayer

ONE: Our gifts bring us together in the name of Jesus Christ.

ALL: **Together we will worship joyfully.**
       Together we will learn through questioning.
       Together we will care compassionately.
       Together we will serve our neighbourhood.
       **Together we will serve the stranger and homeless
       person.**
       **Together we will help the needy and deprived women
       and men overseas whose names we will never know.**

ONE: Together you are strong and effective.

ALL: **Together we will know our gifts truly blessed. Amen.**

 **Pastoral Prayer Pattern** *(Luke 4:56–56)*

ONE: The signs of the times speak of struggle.

ALL: **With the determined spirit of Jesus, we will overcome.**

ONE: We see those with addictions struggling to find
       support.

We see children with learning disabilities needing special care.

We see people with non-essential operations waiting for months.

We see those who need expensive drugs forced to use less effective substitutes.

We pray for those who are sick or depressed, and for those without the money to support their family. *(time of silent reflection)*

We pray for those who have lost loved ones, and for those for whom grief won't go away. *(time of silent reflection)*

The signs of the times speak of struggle.

ALL: **With the determined spirit of Jesus, we will overcome.**

ONE: The signs of the times speak of struggle.

ALL: **With the determined spirit of Jesus, we will overcome.**

ONE: God sees our struggling relationships and friendships.

God sees our concern for the fast passing of our human existence.

God sees those broken dreams that we can't share with a soul.

God sees our procrastination and laziness.

God sees our unspoken longings.

The signs of the times speak of struggle.

ALL: **With the determined spirit of Jesus, we will overcome.**

Commissioning

ONE: Rejoice in your ability to serve.

ALL: **In giving and not in hoarding, we will know God with us.**

In sharing and not in keeping, we will know God with us.

In helping and not in counting hours, we will know God with us.

In friendship and not in rejection, we will know God with us.

ONE: God encourages your generosity.

ALL: **God discourages the mean-spirit.**
We will serve those who Jesus would have served.

Sunday between August 21 and 27 inclusive

Proper 16 [21]

Jeremiah 1:4–10
Psalm 71:1–6
Hebrews 12:18–29
Luke 13:10–17

Jesus heals... the hypocrisy of the synagogue official

Call to Worship *(Jeremiah 1:4–10)*

ONE: Ready or not, we come to worship

ALL: **and God accepts us just as we are.**

ONE: We come feeling the weight of our age and physical limitations, and we come as those who are on top of the world.

ALL: **We come as those prepared through prayer and as those who have not thought to pray.**

ONE: We come as those who have much on our minds from the past week, and we come as those whose spirits are focused and centred.

ALL: **We come open to hear the Word of God for ourselves and for our faith community, and we come distracted and uncertain.**

ONE: Ready or not, we come to worship,

ALL: **and God accepts us just as we are.**

Opening Prayer

ONE: Wonderful acts of health-bringing and healing

ALL: **are signs that you are with us, loving God.**

ONE: Wonderful signs of hope in the midst of despair

ALL: **make clear that you are with us, loving God.**

ONE: Wonderful signs of cooperation in this faith community

ALL: **reveal your presence with us, loving God.**

ONE: Wonderful moves to recognize and help the troubled

ALL: **show that you will stay with us, loving God.**

ONE: Your name is wonderful, loving God.

ALL: **We praise your name. Amen.**

A Prayer of Priorities *(from Luke 13:16)*

ONE: Living God, you call us to keep our priorities straight as Jesus did.

ALL: **Where medical treatment is needed, you call us to insist that it is carried out in a thorough and timely way.**

ONE: You call us to keep our priorities straight.

ALL: **Where children are ignored or forgotten, you call us to insist that their needs are taken seriously.**

ONE: You call us to keep our priorities straight.

ALL: **Where there is conflict at home or in the faith community, you call us to insist that the issues are faced and resolved.**

ONE: You call us to keep our priorities straight.

ALL: **Where need is overwhelming, people starving and homeless in *(current situation)*, you call us to insist that the government has a part to play as one of the global guardians of Earth's people.**

ONE: Living God, you call us to keep our priorities straight as Jesus did. *(time of silent reflection)*

An Assurance that with God We Are Secure

ONE: In all the twists and turns of life,

ALL: **you, loving God, are our rock-solid foundation.**

ONE: When we are apathetic or uncertain, you call us to action.

ALL: **You, loving God, are our rock-solid foundation.**

ONE: When we hang back from trying a new way, a fresh approach, you tell us to get going.

ALL: **You, loving God, are our rock-solid foundation.**

ONE: When we try to put the blame on another person, you remind us to consider our own responsibility.

ALL: **You, loving God, are our rock-solid foundation.**

ONE: When we say that we have reached the limit of our ability, you point us to the cross on the hillside.

ALL: **You, loving God, are our rock-solid foundation. In your security, we have nothing to fear. Amen.**

Offering Prayer

ONE: Rejoice! Your gifts bring closer the realm of God.

ALL: **As we listen and learn,**
as we pray and meditate,
as we care with compassion,
as we give to the hungry,
as we stand beside the bereaved,
as we protest with the humiliated,
as we help the refugee find a home,

ONE: the realm of God comes closer.

ALL: **Thanks be to God for the opportunity to offer gifts. We are blessed. Amen.**

 ### Pastoral Prayer Pattern

ONE: You call us to live with common sense, Holy One –

ALL: **a simple, straightforward attitude for our time.**

ONE: We will keep the planet safe from development and air and water pollution for the sake of our children and our grandchildren.
We will find room in our country for those who are persecuted and abused in their homeland.
We will have equal opportunity for both women and men in business, government, and in traditionally gender-based occupations.
We will accept male nurses and female engineers.
We will refuse to believe that force of arms is better than peacemaking when disputes are to be resolved.
You call us to live with common sense, Holy One –

ALL: **a simple, straightforward attitude for our time.**

ONE: You call us to live with common sense, Holy One –

ALL: **a simple, straightforward attitude for our time.**

ONE: We will advocate to ensure that lifesaving drugs are available to all who need them, without regard to their ability to pay.

We will find practical ways of easing the burden of those who care for men and women suffering from dementia.

We will find practical ways of easing the burden of those who need care for their children while they are working.

We will make sure that those who are without family or good friends eat enough food when they are in hospitals and long-stay institutions.

We will visit those who are sick or depressed, but will not over-stay our visits.

We will be there for as long as it takes for those who have lost loved ones.

You call us to live with common sense, Holy One –

ALL: **a simple, straightforward attitude for our time.**

Commissioning

ALL: **We go from here knowing the rules but, like Jesus, ready to beak them with compassion.**

We go from here aware of the rules but ready to write new rules that are just.

We go from here comfortable with the rules but ready to dream of new rules for the downhearted and discouraged.

We go from here mindful of the rules but ready to partner with those for whom the rules are restricting and humiliating.

Sunday between August 28 and September 3 inclusive

Proper 17 [22]

Jeremiah 2:4–13
Psalm 81:1, 10–16
Hebrews 13:1–8, 15–16
Luke 14:1, 7–14

It is good to practice humility

Call to Worship *(from Luke 14:12–14)*

ONE: We are not worthy to come to this service of worship, glorious God,

ALL: **but you have graciously called us.**

ONE: This is the place where the community of faith gathers to learn, listen, and serve,

ALL: **and you will unfailingly bless us.**

ONE: This is the place where there is prayer offered for the sick and the bereaved,

ALL: **and you will show us how we can help them.**

ONE: This is the place where the poor, hungry and vulnerable will know welcome,

ALL: **and we rejoice and will graciously share as we are able.**

Opening Prayer *(from Jeremiah 2:5)*

ONE: Some worship the mighty dollar,

ALL: **but you, O God, are not with them.**

ONE: Some worship status and political standing,

ALL: **but you, O God, are not with them.**

ONE: Some worship a superior intellect and book learning,

ALL: **but you, O God, are not with them.**

ONE: But where a single mother searches for a home,
where a young person searches for self-esteem,
where an unemployed person searches for a job,
where a family member with dementia searches for
peace,

ALL: **there you will be worshipped, compassionate God.
Amen.**

A Prayer of Learning *(from Psalm 25:4–14)*

ONE: Teach us your ways, O God,

ALL: **and we will live according to your truth.**

ONE: God's way is to act compassionately.

ALL: **We will be there for those in trouble or distress.**

ONE: God's way is to practice humility.

ALL: **We will be there for those who have hit rock bottom.**

ONE: God's way is to forgive thoroughly.

ALL: **We will be there for those who have hurt us badly.**

ONE: God's way is to love generously.

ALL: **We will be there for those who have been despised and
alienated.** *(time of silent reflection)*

Assurance of Going God's Way

ONE: Even when we are pressured,

ALL: **we will go God's way.**

ONE: Even when the path ahead is troubled,

ALL: **we will go God's way.**

ONE: Even when we lose support and assistance,

ALL: **we will go God's way.**

ONE: Even when are directly challenged,

ALL: **we will go God's way.**

ONE: And when we are ready to throw in the towel,

ALL: **still, we will go God's way.**

ONE: God's loving strength will hold you up,

ALL: **and in the resolution of Jesus Christ you will joyfully
endure. Amen.**

Offering Prayer

ONE: We bring these gifts to be blessed, so that change will become reality.

ALL: **With these gifts, the hungry will be fed.**
With these gifts, the sick will be visited.
With these gifts, the Good News will be shared.
With these gifts, the humble will be given confidence.
With these gifts, the arrogant will be put in their place.
With these gifts, the crucified will be loved.
With these gifts, those far from here will be nurtured.

ONE: Accept these gifts, O God. Bless the givers and those who gracefully receive.

ALL: **In Jesus' name, Amen.**

 ### Pastoral Prayer Pattern

ONE: God's people are a hospitable people.

ALL: **We will practice hospitality.**

ONE: We will welcome the stranger carefully.
We will eat and talk together joyfully.
We will speak of own needs when necessary and attend to the needs of the downhearted with sensitivity.
We will look to the needs of those outside our faith community with responsibility.
God's people are a hospitable people.

ALL: **We will practice hospitality.**

ONE: God's people are a hospitable people.

ALL: **We will practice hospitality.**

ONE: Our hearts will be open to receive the deepest concerns.
Our homes will be a sanctuary of refreshment and calm.
Our minds will be ready to work on the challenges that divide and dispute.

Our spirits will be in tune with God's way of love.
God's people are a hospitable people.

ALL: **We will practice hospitality.**

Commissioning *(from Luke 14:10)*

ALL: **There is honour in making way for the humblest.**
There is honour in giving up your place to a poor person.
There is honour in caring for the neediest.
You gain respect in working for the challenged ones.
You gain respect in seeking freedom for those who are captives.
You gain respect in pursuing training for those who lack skills.
It is through honest reflection that you gain self-worth.
It is through modesty that you gain good friends.
It is through facing struggles that you gain the peace of Christ.

Sunday between September 4 and 10 inclusive

Proper 18 [23]

Jeremiah 18:1–11
Psalm 139:1–6, 13–18
Philemon 1–21
Luke 14:25–33

The potter and the clay, the cost of discipleship

Call to Worship

ONE: We come to worship you, living God,

ALL: and you welcome us.

ONE: We come to worship you, living God,

ALL: and you accept us.

ONE: We come to worship you, living God,

ALL: and you bring us together to support each other.

ONE: We come to worship you, living God,

ALL: and you bring us together to serve.

ONE: We come to worship you, living God,

ALL: and you bring us together to receive help.

ONE: We come to worship you, living God,

ALL: and in life and beyond life, your love is always with us.

Opening Prayer

ALL: Loving God,

ONE: if our Christian faith costs us time and effort,

ALL: we will gladly give both to follow Jesus.

ONE: If our Christian faith costs us friends and
acquaintances,

ALL: **we will gladly give both to follow Jesus.**

ONE: If our Christian faith costs us prestige and status,

ALL: **we will gladly give both to follow Jesus.**

ONE: If our Christian faith costs us lifestyle or life direction,

ALL: **we will look to the cross and remember what faithfulness cost Jesus. Amen.**

Prayer of Thanksgiving after the Summer Break

ONE: For a time of reunion with family members,

ALL: **we thank you, loving God.**

ONE: For a time visiting with old friends and making new ones,

ALL: **we thank you, loving God.**

ONE: For a time of rest and relaxation,

ALL: **we thank you, loving God.**

ONE: For a time of exploring new places and revisiting the old and the familiar,

ALL: **we thank you, loving God.**

ONE: For this time of new beginnings in church *(and children's group)*,

ALL: **we thank you, loving God.**

ONE: Bless our time together

ALL: **as we joyfully strive to be your faithful people. Amen.**

A Prayer for the Holy Potter to Shape us and Mold Us *(from Jeremiah 18:1–11)*

ONE: Wonderful Potter, we come before you as clay on the wheel. Shape us and mold us.

ALL: **Shape us as those who are not just enthusiastic listeners, but who are active doers of good.**

ONE: Mold us as those who do not simply see injustice, but who go out of the way to right wrongs.

ALL: **Shape us as those who do not just talk about helping the vulnerable, but who get started.**

ONE: Mold us as those who not only pledge our commitment to Jesus Christ, but who are ready to feed the hungry, shelter the homeless and work to free the prisoners.

ALL: **Shape us as faithful followers of Jesus; mold us as caregivers and fellow adventurers of the faith community.** *(time of silent reflection)*

Assurance of Use by the Holy Potter

ONE: In the hands of the Holy Potter, you can be changed, you can be reshaped, you can be remolded.

ALL: **We are ready to let the Holy Potter go to work with us. The Potter lets us put the past behind us. The Potter will use us regardless of age or status or gender. The Potter will use each talent that is ours. With the Potter there is no time that is inconvenient. The Potter accepts our church friends and our non-church friends just as they are.**

ONE: As the clay can be transformed, so you will be transformed.

ALL: **And the Holy Potter will rejoice. Amen.**

Offering Prayer *(from Psalm 139)*

ONE: You are with us all the time, loving God. You never leave us, and by your presence we are blessed.

ALL: **Our gifts are one way of thanking you. Our compassionate acts are another way. But whether giving or receiving, we are yours.**

ONE: Bless what we have given this morning, and bless what we have received in our worship,

ALL: **that within this faith community, within the neighbourhood, and in nations far from here, people will know your love at work, and rejoice. Amen.**

 ### Pastoral Prayer Pattern

ONE: When your glorious order is established, living God,

ALL: **the last shall be first, and the first shall be last.**

ONE: The hungry will be fed and those without a home will
       be promptly offered one.
       We pray for those without food or permanent shelter
       No child will go to bed hungry or to school without
       lunch.
       We pray for children who go without food or who are
       forced to work.
       Those with mental challenges will get the help they
       need, and those with physical challenges will be able to
       go wherever they want.
       The much-criticized prophets, who speak out for a
       healthy planet Earth, will be given honour and respect.
       When your glorious order is established, living God,

ALL: **the last shall be first, and the first shall be last.**

ONE: When your glorious order is established, living God,

ALL: **the last shall be first, and the first shall be last.**

ONE: The least visible faith community members will be seen
       as loved and vital to the church. They will be visited.
       Thorough training will be provided to each member
       who volunteers for local faith community tasks.
       The voices of children will be heard and their opinions
       taken to heart.
       The needs of national and international projects,
       which depend on gifts from the mission fund, will be
       joyfully met.
       When your glorious order is established, living God,

ALL: **the last shall be first, and the first shall last.**

Commissioning

ONE: Go from here with humility.

ALL: **We seek understanding and not status.**
       We seek to help the poor and to counter the power of
       those who have so much.
       We seek to enable learning rather than to show off

what we have learned.
We seek good friends and seek to be a good friend.

ONE: Accept the thanks you are given and be ready to be a good thanks-giver.

Accept the challenges that come to you and be ready to challenge others.

Accept the wonderful gifts of God and be ready to gracefully give to those who need God's gifts.

Sunday between September 11 and 17 inclusive

Proper 19 [24]

Jeremiah 4:11–12, 22–28
Psalm 14
1 Timothy 1:12–17
Luke 15:1–10

The parable of the lost sheep and the lost coin

Call to Worship

ONE: We may come to this service as losers,

ALL: **but we will return home as winners.**

ONE: We may not see the way ahead clearly,

ALL: **but here we will receive a fresh direction.**

ONE: We may not easily brush off our apathy,

ALL: **but here we will receive spiritual energy.**

ONE: We may not commit ourselves as followers of Christ,

ALL: **but here we will receive fresh inspiration.**

ONE: We cannot forget what brought Jesus to crucifixion,

ALL: **but from now on we will live in the power of resurrection.**

Opening Prayer *(from 1 Timothy 1:12)*

ONE: We give thanks to Christ as we meet in faith community,

ALL: **and we are strengthened.**

ONE: We give thanks to Christ as we meet in faith community,

ALL: **and we are encouraged.**

ONE: We give thanks to Christ as we meet in faith community,

ALL: **and we know that radical change is possible.**

ONE: We give thanks to Christ as we meet in faith community,

ALL: **and we are certain that God's grace will overcome our fear. Amen.**

A Prayer of God's Constant Presence

ONE: In the ups and downs of life, you are with us, Holy One.

ALL: **When life is going well and we are happy, you celebrate with us.**

ONE: When life is tough and we are on our own, you stay with us.

ALL: **You are with us in those moments of despair and disappointment.**

ONE: You are with us in the joyful company of family and friends.

ALL: **When illness comes from nowhere, you will not leave us.**

ONE: And when recovery comes slowly but surely, you are with us for the long haul.

ALL: **Ever-present God, you are our companion.**
You will never leave us or give up on us. *(time of silent reflection)*

Assurance of Renewal and Joy

ONE: Sometimes loss comes to us suddenly, and sometimes we bring loss on ourselves.

ALL: **We lose a loved one through death.**
We lose a good friend because she moves away.
We lose the friendship of a colleague through an ill-chosen remark.

ONE: We know we may offer our losses to you, Holy One, and we know you will be with us as we come to terms with them,

ALL: **so that in the empathy of a compassionate one, in social media contact over the miles, and in a sincere apology, there is hope of renewal, and the path to joy is opened. Amen.**

Offering Prayer

ONE: Why do we give?

ALL: **We give to deepen our life of faith.**
We give because the life of faith is vital to us, and is expressed in our worship, our learning, and our acts of compassion.
We give to deepen the life and influence of our faith community.
We give to breathe life into faith communities throughout this nation and far beyond our shores through the mission fund.
We give so that the just voice may be heard.

ONE: Bless these gifts, loving God, in the name of Jesus who in faithfulness gave his life. Amen.

Pastoral Prayer Pattern

ONE: We look carefully and persistently for that which is most worthwhile.

ALL: **And you bless our search, Holy One.**

ONE: We search patiently and carefully for ways our friends can reduce their level of pain.
We search for ways to motivate the government to increase the payments made to those who rely on social assistance.
Compassionately we search for ways to find and support those in our faith community who are suffering.
Compassionately we search for ways to stand beside those who have lost loved ones and those who feel the numbness of bereavement.
Compassionately we are open to the deepest feelings of those who no longer think their life has worth.

Compassionately we are open to the deepest feelings of those who are unhappy in foster and group homes. We look carefully and persistently, for that which is most worthwhile.

ONE: **And you bless our search, Holy One.**

ONE: We look carefully and persistently for that which is most worthwhile.

ALL: **And you bless our search, Holy One.**
We search at each new stage of life for work that is fulfilling.
We search at each new stage of life for interests that are challenging.
We search at each stage of life for those things that resonate with our faith.
We search for relationships and friendships that are good for us and that are good for the other person.
We search for ways in which we can affect the climate of our planet, our neighbourhood, and the suffering of our world.
We look carefully and persistently for that which is most worthwhile.

ALL: And you bless our search, Holy One.

Commissioning

ONE: The lost has been found. Go with joy.

ALL: **Find the most precious aspect of your life's journey and rejoice as you grow in it.**
Find the relationships that enable you to blossom, and put behind you those that restrict and deny freedom.
Find out who you can help through your generosity, and who through their generosity are able to help you.
Find out the ways in which you can serve your neighbours, and be open to their care for you and your loved ones.
The lost has been found. Rejoice!

Sunday between September 18 and 24 inclusive

Proper 20 [25]

Jeremiah 8:18 – 9:1
Psalm 79:1–9
1 Timothy 2:1–7
Luke 16:1–13

The parable of the dishonest steward

Call to Worship

ONE: The music of this faith community

ALL: fills us with joy and enables our praise to take wing.

ONE: The friendly conversation we enjoy

ALL: keeps us in touch and allows us to give and receive support.

ONE: The Word we hear

ALL: challenges us to act justly and gives us peace in the struggle.

ONE: The pattern of Jesus before us

ALL: roots us in compassion and inspires us to change our world for good.

or

ONE: Friends, find fresh possibilities through worship.

ALL: In prayer we will find a calm place and a voice that calls us to act.

ONE: Friends, know community through worship.

ALL: We will know fellowship and support in this place.

ONE: Friends, know inspiration through worship.

ALL: **Through the Good News proclaimed, we will be changed.**

ONE: Friends, know challenge through worship.

ALL: **With the life's pattern of Jesus before us, we will find our way.**

Opening Prayer

ONE: Loving God,

ALL: **this is the time of worship.**

ONE: This is a holy time.

ALL: **Through worship we humbly approach our Creator.**

ONE: This is a time of gathering together.

ALL: **Through worship we are strengthened in faith community.**

ONE: This is a time to give thanks.

ALL: **Through worship our thanksgiving is given words and music.**

ONE: This is the time to reflect and pray.

ALL: **Through worship the deepest part of us is touched and secured.**

ONE: This is the time to listen for your Word for us.

ALL: **Through worship we are encouraged to hear and to act. Amen.**

A Prayer of Decisive Action

ONE: Loving God,

ALL: **you call us from inaction to action,**
from procrastination to getting busy,
from talking about what we will do, to doing it.
We *will* help our neighbour.
We *will* be there for our children and our grandchildren.
We *will* use our talents in the faith community.
We *will* help the stranger in our midst.
We *will* learn about and speak out against the destruction of our planet.

ONE: And you, loving God, *will* keep us from finding excuses to do nothing. *(time of silent reflection)*
Loving and active God,

ALL: **we thank you. Amen**

Assurance of God's Concern for Us and Our World

ONE: It is there in the words of the prophets, there in the words of the ancient leaders of Israel, and in the words and acts of Jesus, that you, Holy One, care passionately for your people, and that includes *us*.

ALL: **You are our rock-solid foundation.**
You are our shelter from the storm.
You are our focus for learning.
You are the voice that speaks against injustice.
You are the call to action.
You are persistence when hard times come.
You, Holy One, are ours and we are yours. Amen.

Offering Prayer

ONE: Your gifts make opportunities possible through this faith community.
You are God's people.
God's people may gather together

ALL: **for praise and prayer.**

ONE: God's people may gather together

ALL: **to learn and reflect.**

ONE: God's people may gather together

ALL: **to care for the sick and the bereaved.**

ONE: God's people may gather together

ALL: **to work for Christ in this neighbourhood.**

ONE: God's people may gather together

ALL: **to support the homeless and the suffering in our world.**
It is good to gather together as God's people.
It is good to give so this can happen. Amen.

Pastoral Prayer Pattern

ONE: We are a people on the move.

ALL: **Inspire us, Holy Spirit.**

ONE: We are tired of the inaction on climate change.

We deplore the suppression of news and the distortion of news.

We despise the invisible barriers that prevent women from reaching their potential.

We are tired of the excuses for Indigenous people being denied clean water and warm and waterproof homes.

We distrust politicians whose vote can be bought by campaign donations.

We are a people on the move.

ALL: **Inspire us, Holy Spirit.**

ONE: We are a people on the move.

ALL: **Inspire us, Holy Spirit.**

ONE: We will encourage the sharing of our Christian resources with other churches.

We will find ways to make scriptures speak clearly for today's people.

We will find joy in music that makes our body shake and our feet tap.

We will invite the neighbourhood in to share in all that satisfies us and makes us happy.

We will be open to the truth that is within the sacred writings of other faiths.

We will have the spirit of Jesus joyfully breaking out in all we do.

We are a people on the move.

ALL: **Inspire us, Holy Spirit.**

Commissioning

ONE: Work with urgency; you are called to be about God's
      work.

      Speak up for the downtrodden and poor.

ALL: **We will call on our leaders to care for them.**

ONE: Stand beside the sick and the bereaved.

ALL: **We will count them among our good friends.**

ONE: Be aware of the youngest and most at risk.

ALL: **We will guard their rights and attend to their needs.**

ONE: Reflect on those challenges and concerns that are your
      own.

ALL: **We will take the time to reflect on our needs and how
      they can be met.**

ONE: And when the burdens of the world rest on our
      shoulders, we will offer them to God, for God's
      graceful care.

Sunday between September 25 and October 1 inclusive

Proper 21 [26]

Jeremiah 32:1–3a, 6–15
Psalm 91:1–6, 14–16
1 Timothy 6:6–19
Luke 16:19–31

A story of the huge divide between the rich and the poor

Call to Worship

ONE: Come and worship with us.

ALL: **Some of us are poor and some are rich.**

ONE: You are welcome however much money you have or don't have.

ALL: **Some of us are in the best of health and some of us are struggling.**

ONE: You are welcome if you are at peak fitness and you are welcome if you have mental or physical challenges.

ALL: **Some of us are gay, some of us are straight, and some of us are trans.**

ONE: You are welcome whatever your sexual orientation.

ALL: **Some of us are committed to Jesus through baptism, some of us are searchers.**

ONE: You are welcome wherever your faith journey has led you so far.

ALL: **We are happy to be here.**

Opening Prayer

ONE: We are here to witness to the love Christ shown,

ALL: **and we joyfully give thanks for that love.**

ONE: We see that love at work as one church friend helps another,

ALL: **and the community of faith is built up.**

ONE: We see that love at work as the sick are visited and the bereaved comforted.

ALL: **Compassion is alive and practiced.**

ONE: We see that love at work when we share friendship and resources with other faith groups,

ALL: **and we grow as we learn from each other.**

ONE: The love of Christ will touch us personally and strengthen us as a faith community.

ALL: **We joyfully give thanks for that love. Amen.**

A Prayer of Hope against Hope

(from Jeremiah 3:6–15)

ONE: We see that money to reduce carbon emissions to safe levels is not sufficient,

ALL: **and we hope against hope that the leaders of the world will consider the state of Mother Earth and the needs of their children and grandchildren.**

ONE: We see more and more refugees pouring over the borders and the resources to house them increasingly strained,

ALL: **and we hope against hope that a warm welcome will replace bleak living conditions, barbed wire, and guard dogs.**

ONE: We see women assaulted and abused with little legal or practical help,

ALL: **and we hope against hope that authorities will have a change of heart so that justice is accorded to all women.**

ONE: We see less and less money provided to help single-parent families receive adequate food and housing,

ALL: and we hope against hope that the huge divide between rich and poor will be closed and that all will share a good basic standard of living. *(time of silent reflection)*

Assurance of a Faithful World

ONE: With God all things are possible, and we rejoice.

ALL: **We believe no child will go to bed hungry.**
We believe that Mother Earth will be set on the course to health.
We believe that refugees will find permanent homes.
We believe that gender equality will be attained.
We believe that the rich will come to give from their plenty to support those without means of livelihood.

ONE: Bless our efforts to help the neediest, O God.
Bless us as we strive to get by with insufficient resources, O God.

ALL: **Amen.**

Offering Prayer

ONE: We offer from our riches and we offer from what little we have, but we know that you, loving God, bless our gifts, large and small alike.
We give and we remember.

ALL: **We remember those of our faith community who are sick or who are tried and tested by life's struggles.**
We remember our minister/pastor and those who lead and care for our church.
We remember those of other faith groups who meet and work with us.
We remember those who will receive renewal and hope because of our gifts to the mission fund, some in this country, some overseas.

ONE: Loving God, bless this money as it goes to work for good, in the name and the way of Jesus.

ALL: **Amen.**

Pastoral Prayer Pattern

ONE: Can the gap be closed between rich and poor?

ALL: **We will work so that all people receive what they need for dignified living.**

ONE: As we study the concept of a minimum wage for all people;

as the very rich are taxed so that the very poor can be helped;

as we speak out for the voiceless – children, the old and infirm, those with mental challenges;

as we demand medical services for those who have to wait;

as we remember those we love who are going through hard times – naming in particular…holding them up before you, loving God;

as we call for grief groups to support those who have been bereaved and as we are present for those who grieve;

so we are trying hard to bring the "have-nots" and the "haves" closer together.

Can the gap be closed between rich and poor?

ALL: **We will work so that all people receive what they need for dignified living.**

ONE: Can the gap be closed between rich and poor?

ALL: **We will work so that all people receive what they need for dignified living.**

ONE: Some of us are in a position to give from our plenty and we are called to share our resources with those who have little.

Some of us have nothing and need basic resources to keep our children healthy and warm in winter.

We are called to work together so that people in authority are aware of those needs and do their best to meet them.

We look at our own country, and we look at nations throughout the world.

From the faces of starving children, from the hovels in which some must be brought up, from the lack of clean water and medical services, obscene inequality shouts at us for justice.

Can the gap be closed between rich and poor?

ALL: **We will work so that all people receive what they need for dignified living.**

Commissioning

ONE: Be ready to speak out for the poor. Be ready to declare your poverty. Be ready to speak to the powerful about ending poverty. Be ready to work with your brothers and sisters for increased social benefits and better housing. Be ready for opposition from those who want to keep what they have in the bank. Be ready to support political parties that have a compassionate approach to wealth.

ALL: **With the help of God, we are ready.**

Sunday between October 2 and 8 inclusive

Proper 22 [27]
sometimes celebrated as
Worldwide Communion Sunday

Lamentations 1:1–6
Lamentations 3:19–26
or Psalm 137
2 Timothy 1:1–14
Luke 17:5–10

Faith is the most powerful force in the whole world

Call to Worship *(from Luke 17:7–10)*

ONE: Nothing special about us,

ALL: **we are God's ordinary people meeting together.**

ONE: But God blesses our meeting and gives us a joy that is extra-ordinary.

ALL: **In our prayer and in our praise, we thank our Creator.**

ONE: In our listening to the scriptures, we receive encouragement, hope, and a fresh direction.

ALL: **In our Holy Communion, we are one as we eat bread, drink wine, and remember the life and death of Jesus.**

ONE: As you care for one another, you will know true fellowship.

ALL: **As we care for the poor and the fragile we will know joy.**

ONE: And as you prepare to return to our small part of the world, you will be strengthened and emboldened.

ALL: **We are God's ordinary people, but we are people of faith to be reckoned with.**

Opening Prayer *(2 Timothy 2:1–14)*

ONE: There are many gifts of the Spirit as we come to worship.

ALL: **There is the gift of thanksgiving for our friends in Jesus Christ.**

ONE: There are many gifts of the Spirit:

ALL: **the gifts of power and love and self-discipline.**

ONE: There are many gifts of the Spirit:

ALL: **the gift of the Good News, to proclaim and to put into effect.**

ONE: There are many gifts of the Spirit:

ALL: **the gift of hope in Jesus, crucified but risen.**

ONE: There are many gifts of the Spirit:

ALL: **gifts to treasure, gifts to rely on, but above all gifts to use faithfully in the service of Jesus the Christ. Amen.**

A Prayer of Faith

ONE: What does it mean to be God's faithful people?

ALL: **We will meet regularly, pray with hope, and be ready to meet need.**

ONE: Will you have the resources you need?

ALL: **Between us, we have many skills and talents. We will share our gifts and work for the common good.**

ONE: Will you go to work?

ALL: **We will work within this faith community, we will be aware of neighbourhood needs, and we will give to help those far from here, whose names we do not know.**

ONE: Who will be your pattern and guide?

ALL: **We have the life, death and rising of Jesus to guide us, and the story of his followers down the ages to inspire us.**

ONE: You have nothing to fear. Go in peace.

ALL: **God's Spirit will go with us.** *(time of silent reflection)*

Assurance of Faithful Persistence

ONE: Loving God,

ALL: **you call on us to persist.**

ONE: Even if the task seems more difficult than you first thought,

ALL: **we will not be discouraged.**

ONE: Even if you feel you don't have the skills for the task,

ALL: **we will find others with the necessary skills.**

ONE: Even if the time for finishing the task is not long enough,

ALL: **we will do as much as we are able.**

ONE: Even if others downplay your abilities,

ALL: **we will keep on going; maybe they will help.**

ONE: It seems that there is nothing that cannot be overcome.

ALL: **With faith, nothing is impossible. Amen.**

Offering Prayer

ONE: We give

ALL: **believing we can make a difference.**

ONE: We give

ALL: **for our common gifts, of money, talent, bread and wine are powerful symbols of what we can achieve together.**

ONE: We give

ALL: **for our local faith community, but also for the neighbourhood and the overseas work of the church.**

ONE: We give

ALL: **of our time and our talents in Christ's service.**

ONE: And we receive

ALL: **joy, as we realize how effective our gifts have proved to be.**

ONE: And we receive

ALL: **your blessing, loving God, as our gifts are used to meet so many needs in the name of Jesus. Amen.**

Pastoral Prayer Pattern

ONE: We bring our faith with us to the holy table,

ALL: **for with faith the barriers are broken down.**

ONE: The hungry are able to receive food from those who
have plenty.

Those denied a place to sleep will find a room in from
the cold.

The climate-change prophets will know the joy of
being heard.

The peacemakers will get results.

Those who are in prison will receive education and
emotional counselling instead of punishment.

We bring faith with us to the holy table,

ALL: **for with faith the barriers are broken down.**

ONE: We bring our faith with us to the holy table,

ALL: **for with faith the barriers are broken down.**

ONE: We will no longer see those of other faiths as people to
be evangelized, but as people who have important faith
concepts to add to our own.

We will no longer be worried by the noise of children
playing during the service, but welcome their lively
presence and be tested by their simple but profound
questions.

We will no longer automatically accept everyone and
anyone willing to fill volunteer positions in the faith
community, but will insist on the necessary police
checks and training.

We will insist that the confidence of those we pray for
in church is maintained.

We bring our faith with us to the holy table,

ALL: **for with faith the barriers are broken down.**

Commissioning

ONE: You go from here as Christ's faithful servants.

ALL: **We will serve by building up the community of faith.**
We will serve by confronting the leaders and power brokers.
We will serve by valuing the very old, the very young, and the downhearted.
We will serve by doing as well as by talking.
We will serve by prayer, meditation and reading the scriptures.

ONE: As faithful servants of Jesus Christ, there is nothing you cannot achieve.

ALL: **Amen.**

Sunday between October 9 and 15 inclusive

Proper 23 [28]
celebrated as Thanksgiving Sunday in Canada

Jeremiah 29:1, 4–7
Psalm 66:1–12
Timothy 2:8–15
Luke 17:11–19

Thanks from the least expected source, but sincere

Call to Worship

ONE: In our questioning, in our certainty, in our vulnerability, in our hopefulness, we are within this faith community.

ALL: **God will speak and we will listen.**

ONE: With our thankfulness, with our regrets, with our joy, and with our sorrow, we come before the Holy One.

ALL: **God will speak and we will listen.**

ONE: With our resolve, with our uncertainty, with our apathy and with our readiness to get things done, we have come.

ALL: **God will speak and we will listen.**

ONE: This is our meeting place with the Holy One. This is the time that commitment is forged.

ALL: **God will speak, we will listen, and we will begin God's work.**

Opening Prayer

ONE: We look up and we give thanks.

ALL: **In the starry sky, in the gentle rain,**
"The heavens declare the glory of our God."

ONE: We look around and give thanks.

ALL: **The faces of family and the faces of friends speak of God's love, speak of God's closeness to us.**

ONE: We look within this faith community and give thanks.

ALL: **The worship we share and our service in Christ's name tell of our commitment.**

ONE: We look to our neighbourhood and give thanks.

ALL: **Through deeds of caring, through space shared, we make clear the Good News.**

ONE: We look beyond our familiar space and people and give thanks.

ALL: **Through gifts shared, and by our support of the poor and persecuted, your work is done, most loving God. Amen.**

Prayer of Regrets

ONE: As we look back, loving God, we have regrets.

ALL: **We recall words spoken in anger and words spoken that were best left unsaid.** *(time of silent reflection)*

ONE: We give thanks that we can leave these words in the past and start again.

ALL: **We recall actions that hurt friend and stranger, and good deeds left undone.** *(time of silent reflection)*

ONE: We give thanks that we can leave these actions in the past and start again.

ALL: **We recall loved ones ignored and good friends kept at a distance.** *(time of silent reflection)*

ONE: We give thanks that we can be open about our failures and start again.

ALL: **We recall good dreams that did not come to fruition, and missed opportunities for helping others.** *(time of silent reflection)*

ONE: We give thanks that you are a God of wonderful new dreams and that we can let the old ones go. *(time of silent reflection)*

Assurance of a New way

ONE: Loving God, you call us to be open about those ways in which we have hurt others and have gone against your enduring love and compassion.

You will not let us harbour a grudge or keep the fire of resentment smoldering.

ALL: **God promises us peace and opens a new way.**
We are no longer bound by the past.
Thanks be to God. Amen.

Offering Prayer

ALL: **Most loving God, our gifts are thanks-offerings to you.**

ONE: We thank you for this Sunday morning's worship – music, Word, and silence – and for those who lead and take part.

ALL: **We thank you for this church and for its compassionate work in this city/town.**

ONE: We thank you for the work of the wider church and the work our mission offerings support.

ALL: **We thank you for Jesus Christ whose life, death, and rising is at the centre of all we do.**

ONE: Bless our offerings and accept our thanksgiving

ALL: **in the name of Jesus, your chosen one. Amen.**

 ### Pastoral Prayer Pattern

ONE: For those who work so hard to live out God's love for our world,

ALL: **we give thanks.**

ONE: In a world where conflict still rages and refugees cross borders enduring terrible hardships, we give thanks for the peace-bringers and for those who grant refuge.

In a world where the difference between rich and poor is acute, and where many families do not know where their next meal is coming from, we give thanks for those who strive to close the gap and who work so that

no child goes to school, or goes to bed, hungry.
In a world where the rich have the benefits of a
multitude of health services and drugs while the poor
make do with basic care or less, we give thanks for
those who give and who advocate for people who have
so little.
For those who work so hard to live out God's love for
our world,

ALL: **we give thanks.**

ONE: For those who work so hard to live out God's love for
our church,

ALL: **we give thanks.**

ONE: Bless the faith community, O God, that rejoices with a
wide variety of praise and prayer in Sunday worship.
Bless the faith community, O God, that will not be
content until the whole family can be comfortably
welcomed to its worship, learning, and social activities.
Bless the faith community, O God, where those who
are infirm and shut-in are considered a vital part of
community life.
Bless the faith community, O God, whose reach goes
beyond the boundaries of this nation and can call
people in other lands "sister" and "brother."
For those who work so hard to live out God's love for
our church,

ALL: **we give thanks.**

Commissioning

ONE: Go from here as God's thankful people.

ALL: **For our created world and for those who strive to keep
it good, thanks.**
For our birth and for our living, for our loved ones
and our friends, thanks.

For our faith community and for the worship and service that *(name of faith community)* makes possible, thanks.

Thanks beyond all limits, thanks beyond reckoning, thanks beyond any limits of time; heartfelt thanks to our most loving God.

Sunday between October 16 and 22 inclusive

Proper 24 [29]
sometimes celebrated as Peace Sabbath

Jeremiah 31:27–34
Psalm 119:97–104
2 Timothy 3:14 –4:5
Luke 18:1–8

The new covenant and the parable of the widow and the judge.

Call to Worship *(from Jeremiah 31:31–33)*

ONE: The covenant stands, loving God.

ALL: **You are our God and we are your people.**

ONE: The new covenant known by the prophets:

ALL: **you are our God and we are your people.**

ONE: The new covenant made clear by Jesus:

ALL: **you are our God and we are your people.**

ONE: The new covenant witnessed by the saints of the ages:

ALL: **you are our God and we are your people.**

ONE: The new covenant for the faithful ones today:

ALL: **you are our God and we are your people.**

ONE: The covenant stands, loving God.

ALL: **You are our God and we are your people.**

Opening Prayer *(from Psalm 119:97–104)*

ONE: There is wisdom from the scriptures.

ALL: **Within the faith community, we will become wiser.**

ONE: There are fresh insights from the scriptures.

ALL: **Within the faith community, we will see people and events compassionately.**

ONE: There is integrity in the scriptures.

ALL: **Within the faith community, we will follow the faithful way.**

ONE: There is a sense of justice within the scriptures.

ALL: **Within the faith community, we will be on the side of the poor, the vulnerable, and the despised.**

ONE: The Hebrew and Christian scriptures are God's graceful gift to us.

ALL: **Within the faith community, we give thanks wholeheartedly. Amen.**

Prayer for an October Sunday Morning

ONE: The warmth of summer is behind us; fall is our reality.

ALL: **But in or out of season, you are our loving God.**

ONE: The leaves are falling, and the harvest has been gathered from field and garden.

ALL: **And you are eternally faithful, loving God.**

ONE: The mornings are becoming cooler, *tires must be changed, summer clothes put away.*

ALL: **But your love is a constant for us, loving God.**

ONE: The mornings are darker and the light fades sooner,

ALL: **but your Light shines steadily, your Word guides us, and we thank you, loving God. Amen.**

A Prayer of Persistence

ONE: Don't give up; God is with you.

ALL: **When trouble comes, we will not despair.**

ONE: Don't give up; God is with you.

ALL: **When faith is tested, we will endure.**

ONE: Don't give up; God is with you.

ALL: **When friends go their own way, we will respect their reasons.**

ONE: Don't give up; God is with you.

ALL: **When injustice is clear, we will speak and act for the just way.**

ONE: Don't give up; God is with you.

ALL: **God is our companion in the hard places, we will trust God. Amen.**

A Prayer of God's Faithfulness to the Downhearted

ONE: Don't be discouraged if life has treated you badly.

ALL: **In your deepest distress, God stands with you.**

ONE: Don't feel put down if others flaunt their wealth or connections.

ALL: **Though you feel inferior, God stands with you.**

ONE: Don't give up if your compassionate efforts are turned aside.

ALL: **When you are made to feel unnecessary, God stands with you.**

ONE: Don't knuckle under when there is pressure to withdraw support.

ALL: **In renewed support, in the certainty that your cause is just, God stands with you.**

Assurance that God is with the Humble

ONE: Jesus loved the humblest and those who were challenged.
Jesus enjoyed their company:

ALL: **good friend of the poorest,
good friend of the tax collector,
good friend of despised women,
good friend of the physically challenged,
good friend of the mentally ill.**

ONE: For those of us who are humble and challenged, there is joy.
For those of us who are not, there is cause to consider our attitudes. *(time of silent reflection)*

ONE: Loving God, give us the eyes of Jesus as we look at the humble of our world.
Loving God, we who have so little rejoice that you stand with us.

ALL: **Amen.**

Offering Prayer

ONE: Our gifts enable this faith community and faith communities far beyond...*(name of church)* to go about the worship of God and the work of Jesus Christ.

ALL: **Our gifts sustain the worship life of the church.**
Our gifts sustain pastoral care for the infirm and the suffering.
Our gifts enable boys and girls to have fun and to learn about Christian values.
Our gifts enable young men and women to ask the deepest questions.
Our gifts support mission work, both in this country and overseas.
Our gifts can help people today, but will also sustain the life of faith for months and years.
Loving God, bless our gifts. Amen.

❤ Pastoral Prayer Pattern

ONE: Loving God, you call us to face the challenges of life,

ALL: **with grit and determination.**

ONE: When a minor illness develops into a major one,
when a loved one is diagnosed with dementia or an advanced cancer,
when a family member or friend is accidentally hurt,
when a member of this faith community goes through tough times,
when bereavement comes unexpectedly,
we will be there.
We pray for those who are sick.
In our presence, in our listening, in our comfort of loved ones when realities have to be faced, and in the cost to our own peace of mind,
loving God, you call us to face the challenges of life,

ALL: **with grit and determination.**

ONE: Loving God, you call us to face the challenges of life
ALL: **with grit and determination:**
ONE: the challenge of a change in job or vocation,
the challenge of a relationship that is unsteady,
the challenge of a family member in trouble,
the challenge of retirement after a fulfilling work life,
the challenge of a personality clash in a social group,
the challenge of financial insecurity,
the challenge of following a dream.
In all the different circumstances of life you are there,
loving God, and you call us to face the challenges of
life
ALL: **with grit and determination.**

Commissioning

ONE: Go from here as those who will not give up or give in:
ALL: **constant, when the world is changing;**
listened to, when the clamour is loudest;
prepared, when others are uncertain;
Unafraid, when fear reigns;
Steady, when many are wavering;
Compassionate, when others are serving themselves;
Faithful, in times when faith counts for little.
ONE: You go with determination.
You go supporting each other.
You go with love, and God goes with you.

Sunday between October 23 and 29 inclusive

Proper 25 [30]

Joel 2:23–32
Psalm 65
2 Timothy 4:6–8, 16–18
Luke 18:9–14

The wonder of God in creation, the humble tax collector

Call to Worship *(from Psalm 65)*

ONE: On beaches cleared of plastic waste and polystyrene,

ALL: the Creator will be worshipped with joy.

ONE: On rivers free from pollutants, seas cleansed of industrial waste,

ALL: the Creator will be worshipped with joy.

ONE: In coal mines now covered by soil and saplings, and in gold mines where chemicals have been neutralized,

ALL: the Creator will be worshipped with joy.

ONE: Where men and women are determined that the earth will be kept clean and the water pure,

ALL: the Creator will be worshipped with joy.

ONE: Where government leaders are committed to the use of electric vehicles,

ALL: the Creator will be worshipped with joy.

ONE: Where boys and girls create an environment of reusing and recycling,

ALL: the Creator will be worshipped with joy.

Opening Prayer *(from Psalm 65)*

ONE: Sender of the rain, grower of the grain,

ALL: creator and sustainer of creation, we praise you.

ONE: In the smallest plant, in the giant tree,

ALL: **life force and moving Spirit, we glorify you.**

ONE: For the nimble monkey and the lion in the pride,

ALL: **we thank you.**

ONE: For the twisting trout and the breaching whale,

ALL: **we thank you.**

ONE: For the wonderful variety of creation, from a single bacterium to the Milky Way,

ALL: **creator and sustainer of creation, we thank you.**

ONE: And for humankind, who has the choice to keep creation good or to ruin it,

ALL: **we thank you God, creator of us all. Amen.**

A Prayer for Humility

ONE: Keep us on the humble path, loving God.

ALL: **When we want to show our superiority, show us another way.**

ONE: Keep us on the humble path, loving God.

ALL: **Remind us that basic needs go unmet while some have luxuries in abundance.**

ONE: Keep us on the humble path, loving God.

ALL: **Show us the children who go to school hungry.**

ONE: Keep us on the humble path, loving God.

ALL: **Encourage us to talk with people who cannot find work.**

ONE: Keep us on the humble path, loving God.

ALL: **Take us to homes where water must be boiled and the bathroom is outside.**

ONE: Keep us on the humble path, loving God.

ALL: **Encourage us to be with those who have addictions and who are not receiving help.**

ONE: Keep us on the humble path, loving God.

ALL: **Help us contact the leaders who speak for the poor, and those for whom poverty is not a priority.** *(time of silent reflection)*

Assurance that God Will Keep Us Humble

ONE: We have known times when money has been in short supply.

ALL: **We have known times when we have been without work.**

ONE: We have known times when life has been challenging and downright difficult.

ALL: **For some of us, this is the way it is now.** *(time of silent reflection)*

ONE: In our times of strength, in our times of weakness,

ALL: **you go with us, loving God.**
Enable us to accept the care of good friends and to be the trusted companions of others. Amen.

Offering Prayer

An attempt to answer the question, "Why do we give money each time we worship?"

ONE: We offer these gifts to ensure a warm welcome for newcomers.

ALL: **We offer these gifts to praise your name, loving God, and to be aware of your presence in our singing and in our moments of quiet.** *(time of silent reflection)*

ONE: We offer these gifts so that the scriptures may be heard and their message find a ready response.

ALL: **We offer these gifts to provide an atmosphere where children may learn and question.**

ONE: We offer these gifts to ensure that all who are anxious or afraid receive support.

ALL: **We offer these gifts so that those of us who are downtrodden will be given confidence, and those of us who are secure will be challenged.**

ONE: We offer these gifts to ensure that this local faith community is strengthened.

ALL: **We offer these gifts to encourage faith communities in towns and cities far from this place.**

ONE: Loving God, bless these gifts and enable us to use them with wisdom.

ALL: **Amen.**

 Pastoral Prayer Pattern

ONE: Make sure we listen to the humble,

ALL: **for they speak with your voice, loving God.**

ONE: The humble say, "Respond to the needs of children who are forced to work, and of girls who are denied schooling." The humble say, "Allow us to talk to the politicians and leaders; we have needs that go unfulfilled."

The humble say, "Give us the opportunity to train for worthwhile work; we are keen to get started."

Make sure we listen to the humble,

ALL: **for they speak with your voice, loving God.**

ONE: Make sure we listen to the humble,

ALL: **for they speak with your voice, loving God.**

ONE: The humble call us to pray constantly for people who are going through tough times.

The humble remind us of the importance of those who do the small but essential tasks in the faith community.

The humble tell us of those who are housebound or in care homes who need to be visited.

The humble remind us of those far from here who need our mission fund support.

The humble stay with the bereaved and encourage us to do the same.

Make sure we listen to the humble,

ALL: **for they speak with your voice, loving God.**

Commissioning

ONE: Leave this service with humility.

ALL: **We seek to serve quietly.**
      We seek to question carefully.
      We seek to meet suffering compassionately.
      We seek to sustain our environment persistently.
      We seek to encourage gently.
      We seek to pray unceasingly.
      We seek to follow the way of Jesus faithfully.

ONE: God goes with you. God will never leave you.

Sunday between October 30 and November 5 inclusive

Proper 26 [31]
for All Saints' Day prayers see page 280

Habakkuk 1:1–4, 2:1–4
Psalm 119:137–144
2 Thessalonians 1:1–4, 11–12
Luke 19:1–10

Jesus honours Zacchaeus

Call to Worship

ONE: We come to this service full of hope.

ALL: **We hope for inspiration, and the scriptures will be opened for us.**

ONE: We come to this service full of hope.

ALL: **We hope for fellowship, and our friends are all around us.**

ONE: We come to this service full of hope.

ALL: **We hope for a challenge, and deep needs will be presented to us.**

ONE: We come to this service full of hope.

ALL: **We hope to find Jesus Christ, and Christ's way will become clear to us.**

Opening Prayer

ONE: Loving God, we are challenged in our Christian faith.

ALL: **We are challenged to worship, when shopping and visits are more popular.**

ONE: We are challenged in our Christian faith.

ALL: **We are challenged to open the scriptures, when the Internet has all the answers.**

ONE: We are challenged in our Christian faith.

ALL: **We are challenged to be a part of the faith community, when sports and social groups reach out to us.**

ONE: We are challenged in our Christian faith.

ALL: **We are challenged "to do justice, love kindness, and walk humbly with our God," when self-interest is the prevailing way.**

ONE: As Christians, you are challenged,

ALL: **and we will meet the challenge faithfully. Amen.**

Seeking Repentance, a Prayer *(from Luke 19:7–8)*

ONE: Turn us around, O God, and show us another way.

ALL: **When the tasks of getting and spending are first and foremost, remind us of those who need our care and compassion.**

ONE: Turn us around, O God, and show us another way.

ALL: **When the responses of inaction and apathy are the easiest to sustain, encourage us to face the issues and get things done.**

ONE: Turn us around, O God, and show us another way.

ALL: **When we have held grudges and have refused to forgive, change our attitude; help us to let go.**

ONE: Turn us around, O God, and show us another way.

ALL: **When we have been indifferent to the world's needs, give us empathetic action for those at risk, who are the most vulnerable.** *(time of silent reflection)*

Assurance of Going God's Way *(from Luke 19:9)*

ONE: When your will is aligned to God's will, everything is possible.

ALL: **We will take action.**
        We will seek forgiveness.
        We will work with others.
        We will care generously.

We will advocate for the voiceless.
We will give for the world's poorest.

ONE: And change will become reality.

ALL: **Thanks be to God. Amen.**

Offering Prayer

ONE: You have given so that this faith community can praise
and thank our loving God.

ALL: **Our offering will be blessed.**

ONE: You have given so that the sick may be visited and the
lonely find a friend.

ALL: **Our offering will be blessed.**

ONE: You have given so that questions may be welcomed and
the faith explored.

ALL: **Our offering will be blessed.**

ONE: You have given so that forgiveness may be offered and
a new way begun.

ALL: **Loving God, we know that you will bless our offering.
Amen.**

💔 Pastoral Prayer Pattern

ONE: The compassionate spirit of Jesus

ALL: **is joyfully welcomed.**

ONE: Those who have pain that is hard to control, look for
understanding.
Those who cannot find a listening ear, look for sympa-
thy.
Those who find a diagnosis hard to believe, look for
empathy.
Those who can see no end to their illness, look for
courage. *(time of silent reflection)*

*   Those who have lost a loved one, look for a patient
presence.
The compassionate spirit of Jesus

ALL: **is joyfully welcomed.**

ONE: The compassionate spirit of Jesus
ALL: **is joyfully welcomed.**
ONE: In our depression and in our discouragement, we look for a glimmer of hope.
In our failed dreams and in our expectations, we look for the will to try again.
In our joy and in our elation, we look for those who will celebrate with us.
In those areas of our life where we find fulfillment, we are willing to share our feelings and experiences.
The compassionate spirit of Jesus
ALL: **is joyfully welcomed.**

Commissioning *(from the Luke 19:1–10)*

ONE: Are you ready for new directions?
ALL: **We are ready.**
ONE: Are you sensitive to what is just and fair?
ALL: **We know the way to go.**
ONE: Is welcoming a part of your way, part of the way of our church?
ALL: **We are welcoming individuals; we are a welcoming faith community.**
ONE: Are you ready to make amends? Are you ready to be forgiven?
ALL: **We are prepared for a fresh start.**
ONE: You know the embrace of God.
ALL: **The living God be praised.**

Sunday between November 6 and 12 inclusive

Proper 27 [32]

Haggai 1:15b – 2:9
Psalm 145:1–5, 17–21
        or Psalm 98
2 Thessalonians 2:1–5, 13–17
Luke 20:27–38

Sing a new song... Jesus looks beyond the superficial

Call to Worship *(from Psalm 145)*

ONE: The God we worship is a great God.

ALL: **Day by day we will praise and thank our God.**

ONE: We cannot understand the full scope of God's greatness.

ALL: **From generation to generation, we will praise God.**

ONE: Everything that is good and lovely has its roots in God.

ALL: **God knows each of God's creatures through and through.**

ONE: We will sing of God's glory.

ALL: **We will sing of God's compassion.**

ONE: We will remember the countless merciful acts

ALL: **carried out in God's name.**

Opening Prayer *(from Psalm 98)*

ONE: Praise God!

ALL: **We will sing a new song to God, for God has done wonderful things.**

ONE: Praise God!

ALL: **God's ways will bring radical change to the nations.**

ONE: Praise God!

ALL: **God is committed in constant love to God's people.**

ONE: Praise God!

ALL: **We will praise God with songs and joyful shouts.**

ONE: Praise God!

ALL: **With harp and fiddle, with trumpet and horn, we will bring our praise to God.**

ONE: Praise God!

ALL: **"Justice" and "fairness" are God's watchwords for the world. Amen.**

A Prayer of God's Enduring Love

ONE: In the toughest moments of life, when we are searching for a job, a vocation, or a social group,

ALL: **God's love is with us.**

ONE: When we are challenged in a friendship or a relationship,

ALL: **God's love is with us.**

ONE: When we are tested by accident or ill-health,

ALL: **God's love is with us.**

ONE: When the life of faith seems dry and cold,

ALL: **God's love is with us.**

ONE: When our life comes to an end, and a life beyond time beckons,

ALL: **God's love is with us.** *(time of silent reflection)*

God's Love Endures, No Matter What

ONE: Nothing can separate us from God's love.

ALL: **Old age and infirmity won't do it.**

ONE: Nothing can separate us from God's love.

ALL: **Prejudice based on colour, ethnic origin, or sexual orientation won't do it.**

ONE: Nothing can separate us from God's love.

ALL: **Exploitation of the voiceless and vulnerable won't do it.**

ONE: Nothing can separate us from God's love.

ALL: **The holding of grudges, the betrayal of trust won't do it.**
Nothing in all creation can separate us from God's love as we know it in Christ Jesus.
Thanks be to God. Amen.

Offering Prayer

ONE: Your love, O God, goes to work through our offerings:

ALL: **a love that finds expression in praise and prayer,**
a love that meets the needs of our faith community members,
a love that reaches out to help and heal within our town/city,
a love that through the mission fund gives hope to people all over the world,
a love that was expressed in the life of Jesus and that brought him to the cross.

ONE: In your love, O God, our offerings are blessed.

ALL: **Amen.**

 ### Pastoral Prayer Pattern *(from 2 Thessalonians 2:14)*

ONE: Stand firm.

ALL: **We will hold on to the truths we have been taught.**
We have been taught to love our enemies.

ONE: Pray for those who are in conflict in… and support those groups who care for those who have lost their homes or livelihood.

ALL: **We have been taught to have compassion for the poorest.**

ONE: Pray for those who stand beside the downtrodden, and support those who offer practical help and hope.

ALL: **We have been taught to hold those in authority to account.**

ONE: Pray for those who question people in power positions, and we join those who protest injustice and oppression.

Stand firm.
ALL: **We will hold on to the truths we have been taught.**

🏚️: Stand firm.
ALL: **We will hold on to the truths we have been taught.**
We have been taught to worship on Sunday, the first
day of the week.
ONE: We will prepare for our service, sing with joy, and
listen for God's Word for us.
ALL: **We have been taught to build up the body of Christ,**
the church.
ONE: We will offer our gifts of time and talent, and we will be
enthusiastic members of the "Jesus Team."
ALL: **We have been taught to be good disciples and to share**
our faith stories.
ONE: We take time to learn about our faith, and to be
prepared to tell others what we believe.
Stand firm.
ALL: **We will hold on to the truths we have been taught.**

Commissioning
ONE: Be with us, loving God.
ALL: **Be with us as we question and doubt.**
Be with us as we choose and refuse.
Be with us when we feel at our strongest.
Be with us in our lowest moments.
Be with us when uncertainty grips us.
Be with us when our faith is rooted and secure.
ONE: You are with us as we go back to our corner of the
world.
ALL: **You will never leave us, most loving God.**

Sunday between November 13 and 19 inclusive

Proper 28 [33]

Isaiah 65:17–25
Isaiah 12
2 Thessalonians 3:6–13
Luke 21:5–19

Put your fear and anxiety behind you

Call to Worship

ONE: We come to worship full of hope.

ALL: **With music and song we will glorify God.**

ONE: We come to worship ready to share.

ALL: **Our church friends are around us; we will discover their needs.**

ONE: We come to worship as questioning people.

ALL: **The words within the Word will provide answers.**

ONE: We come to worship ready for action.

ALL: **Injustice and bullying will be exposed and overcome.**

ONE: We come to worship ready to give thanks.

ALL: **We look up, we look around, we remember loved ones, and thanksgiving comes easily.**

Opening Prayer *(from Isaiah 65:17–25)*

ONE: Loving God, we want to join with you in creating "new heavens and a new earth":

ALL: **a world where all are secure,
a world where all children are cared for from before birth,**

a world where happiness is the norm,
a world where old folk are respected,
a world where no one lives without a home,
a world where all enjoy the fruits of their labour,
a world where those who disagree can do so peacefully,
a world where the desperately ill can end their own
lives.

ONE: It is a big task recreating the world, but you, loving God, assure us that we have a part to play and that our efforts matter. Amen.

A Prayer of Trust

ONE: Will you trust God in times of personal trial and difficulty?

ALL: **We will trust God.**

ONE: Will you trust God when trouble comes without any warning?

ALL: **We will trust God.**

ONE: Will you trust God when a good friend lets you down?

ALL: **We will trust God.**

ONE: Will you trust God when you let a good friend down?

ALL: **We will trust God.**

ONE: Will you trust God when you are uncertain of your life's direction?

ALL: **We will trust God.**

ONE: Will you trust God when the international scene is stormy?

ALL: **We will trust God.** *(time of silent reflection)*

An Assurance that We Can Always Trust God

ONE: Reliable when others are not,
there for you when loved ones let you down,
the voice of peace in conflict,
the gentle compassionate presence,
the calming influence where there is anger and
resentment,

ALL: **God is to be heeded. God is to be trusted.**
         We will trust God. Amen.

Offering Prayer

ONE: These gifts are saving grace to those who receive them.

ALL: **Our gifts will enable the church to be present to the**
         infirm and housebound.
         Our gifts will bring joy to the youngest and teach them
         about Jesus Christ.
         Our gifts will provide space for community groups to
         meet and enable us to serve the local community.
         Our gifts will bring compassion to the suffering and a
         vision to those who cannot see the way ahead.

ONE: God will bless these gifts as they go to work in the way
         of Jesus. Amen.

 ## Pastoral Prayer Pattern

ONE: In the midst of uncertainty and weakness,

ALL: **we will stand firm.**

ONE: We will stand firm in support of a friend who is sorely
         tested.
         We will stand firm when the local environment is
         threatened.
         We will stand firm when a diagnosis is surprising and
         unexpected.
         We will stand firm when the pain just won't go away.
         We will stand firm when the ache of bereavement just
         won't go away. *(time of silent reflection)*

ONE: In the midst of uncertainty and weakness,

ALL: **we will stand firm.**

ONE: Because of the presence of good people with us, we
         will stand firm.
         Because we are on the side of the poor and despised,
         we will stand firm.

Because we have the vision of each person giving generously from their store of talents, we will stand firm.

Because we believe that God's way will ultimately prevail, we will stand firm.

In the midst of uncertainty and weakness,

ALL: **we will stand firm.**

Commissioning

ONE: Go from here as those ready to stay calm in the storms of life:

ALL: **prepared, when the world is shaking;**
ready, for the faith-challenging situation;
unflinching, when the attack comes home;
unafraid, when opposition is strong;
gentle, when harsh words are spoken;
straightforward, in question and in answer;

ONE: and always looking to the example of Jesus, who knew the worst of times yet remained faithful.

Reign of Christ Sunday

Proper 29 [34]
final Sunday before Advent

Jeremiah 23:1–6
Luke 1:68–79
or Psalm 46
Colossians 1:11–20
Luke 23:33–43

"This is the King of the Jews"

Call to Worship

ONE: We come humbly to worship.

ALL: **We ask that Christ rule in every aspect of our life.**

ONE: We come quietly to worship.

ALL: **We ask that Christ rule in our mind.**

ONE: We come peacefully to worship.

ALL: **We ask that Christ rule in our heart.**

ONE: We come thankfully to worship.

ALL: **We ask that Christ rule in the joys and sorrows of each day.**

ONE: In worship, in service, you will encounter the rule of Christ.

ALL: **Thanks be to God.**

Opening Prayer

ONE: Nailed to the cross, the statement, "This is the King of the Jews."
Some king! No palace, no royal guard.

ALL: **Some king! A caring mother, a ministry of healing.**

ONE: Some king! No throne, no crown.

ALL: **Some king! A message of hope, a message of salvation.**

ONE: Some king! No robes, no edicts.

ALL: **Some king! A courageous attitude, a refusal to give in.**

ONE: Some king! No taxes, no kingdom.

ALL: **Some king! A way of compassion, a way of love.**
Let us worship the one whose reign will never end.
Amen.

A Prayer from the Foot of the Cross

ONE: Loving God, we see the soldiers.

ALL: **They mocked him, they beat him, they humiliated him,**
and in the unseeing and the uncaring, we see ourselves.

ONE: Loving God, we see the women,

ALL: **and in their courage, faithfulness, and devotion, we**
wish we saw ourselves.

ONE: Loving God, we see no disciples,

ALL: **and in their fear, unfaithfulness and anxiety, we see**
ourselves.

ONE: Loving God we see the notice, "King of the Jews,"

ALL: **and we realize that in the reign of Christ, the notions**
of power and authority have been replaced by Christ-
inspired love and justice. *(time of silent reflection)*

A Prayer as We Leave Place of Crucifixion

ONE: Loving God, go with us as we leave the place of
crucifixion, for we take some realities with us as we
move away from that dreadful place.

ALL: **As we move from the cross, we take the simple thought**
that injustice cannot be tolerated.
As we move from the cross, we realize that our faithful
friends may not be the ones we expect.
As we move away from the cross, we see the results of
power that is abused.
As we move away from the cross, we wonder if we
would have taken risks like the women, or played it
safe with Peter.

ONE: We move away from the cross, but that awful image
remains in our mind's eye.

ALL: **Amen.**

Offering Prayer

ONE: We give, and as we give we bring the rule of Christ closer.

ALL: **When Christ rules, the poorest and the most vulnerable will have powerful friends.**

ONE: When Christ rules, the faith community will search out neighbourhood needs and find ways to meet them.

ALL: **When Christ rules, the old and infirm of the church will be cherished members.**

ONE: When Christ rules, every church member will be a teacher and every member a learner.

ALL: **When Christ rules, praise flows wholeheartedly and our giving will bring closer the rule of Christ. Amen.**

 ### Pastoral Prayer Pattern

ONE: We will advance the reign of Christ.

ALL: **The difference will be amazing.**

ONE: There will be hope for those who are bullied because of their sexual orientation.
There will be understanding for addicts who cannot end their addiction.
There will be a fair wage for those who struggle to make ends meet on the minimum rate.
There will be an end to the exploitation of children.
We will advance the reign of Christ.

ALL: **The difference will be amazing.**

ONE: We will advance the reign of Christ.

ALL: **The difference will be amazing.**

ONE: Meditation and quiet reflection will feature in church life.
Long-term leaders of the church will be offered a break to restore and refresh themselves.
There will be mid-week programs as well as Sunday activities for children.

The needs of faith communities served by the mission fund will be as enthusiastically met as local needs. We will advance the reign of Christ.

ALL: **The difference will be amazing.**

Commissioning

ONE: We want the rule of Christ to prevail:

ALL: **beauty where there is drabness,**
dancing where there is inaction,
music where there is talk,
compassion in the place of indifference,
community in the place of self-interest,
peace where conflict rages,
freedom where there is restriction,
self-confidence where there is vulnerability, and
hope where there is despair.

ONE: You will work to bring the rule of Christ closer. You will expose those who have no time for Christ's rule.

Thanksgiving

4th Thursday in November in the U.S.;
2nd Monday in October in Canada
See also Pentecost Proper 23 [28]

Deuteronomy 26:1–11
Psalm 100
Philippians 4:4–9
John 6:25–35

Jesus – the bread of life

Call to Worship *(from Psalm 100)*

ONE: Worship the Holy One with joy.

ALL: **Joy bursts from our singing.**

ONE: God is at the heart of creation.

ALL: **We are God's and God is ours.**

ONE: We come to church filled with thanksgiving,

ALL: **for God is good and there are no limits to God's faithfulness.**

Opening Prayer

ONE: If God, the Creator, had just made every star in every universe,

ALL: **we would have thanked God wonderfully.**

ONE: If God, the Creator, had just made every flower and every tree,

ALL: **we would have thanked God joyfully.**

ONE: If God, the Creator, had just made every animal and every man and every woman,

ALL: **we would have thanked God, limitlessly.**

ONE: If God, the Creator, had just given us the ability to reason and to question, to encourage and to love,

ALL: **we would have thanked God gloriously.**

ONE: But God has given us all this and so much more, and our praise and adoration will never be done. Amen.

A Prayer of Jesus the Bread of Life

ONE: "The one who comes to me will never be hungry.
The one who believes in me will never thirst."
This is the bread, the word of God, in the Hebrew and Christian scriptures.

ALL: **We feast on the Word; we are challenged and find peace.**

ONE: This is the bread; the stories of the saints of the ages.

ALL: **We are inspired by their deeds, we follow their example, we find peace.**

ONE: This is the bread; the leadership of today's faithful ones.

ALL: **They call us to work humbly and carefully with them, and when we walk the way of Jesus we find peace.**

ONE: This is the bread; the call to justice and compassion.

ALL: **When we heed the call and take the risks, we find peace.**

ONE: This is the bread; symbol of an enduring love.

ALL: **In good times and in hard times, that love will lead to peace.** *(time of silent reflection)*

Assurance that We Will Receive the Bread's Nourishment

ONE: "The one who comes to me will never be hungry;
the one who believes in me will never thirst."
God does not limit who can receive the bread of life.

ALL: **We, God's people of this faith community will receive the bread joyfully,
and so will the downhearted and the miserable,
the despised and those without hope,
the sick and the suffering,
those who have lost loved ones,
and those who seek friendship and a community.**

ONE: This bread is the life of the world.
         We will offer the bread, and when we eat the bread we
         will never be hungry again.

ALL: **Thanks be to God! Amen.**

Offering Prayer

ONE: Give thanks for the generous gifts of God, and use
         God's gifts well.

ALL: **We give thanks that these gifts will sustain the poor and
         downhearted.**
         **We give thanks that these gifts will support and
         encourage the members of this faith community.**
         **We give thanks that these gifts will enable us to teach
         and learn from each other.**
         **We give thanks that these gifts will enable the choir to
         sing and the minister to proclaim a message.**
         **We give thanks that because of these gifts the very
         youngest will play and the older ones will remember.**

ONE: You have praise and thankfulness in your hearts!

ALL: **Alleluia! Amen.**

 **Pastoral Prayer Pattern** *(from 1 Thessalonians 5:18)*

ONE: Rejoice always! Pray without ceasing!

ALL: **Give thanks in all circumstances!**

ONE: When there is a research breakthrough in treatment
         for *breast or prostate cancer,* give thanks.
         Where there is a glimmer of hope in a loved one's
         testing illness, give thanks.
         When the reality of a mental illness is faced for the first
         time, give thanks.
         When a friend or loved one is able to share grief over
         the death of a family member, give thanks.
         Rejoice always! Pray without ceasing!

ALL: **Give thanks in all circumstances!**

ONE: Rejoice always! Pray without ceasing!

ALL: **Give thanks in all circumstances!**

ONE: For the gift of a trusted one in a life crisis: give thanks.
For the courage to end a job, a relationship, or an addiction: give thanks.
For an unexpected, joyful surprise: give thanks.
For the spiritual gifts of a faithful life: give thanks.
Give thanks to God, your loving God.
Rejoice always! Pray without ceasing!

ALL: **Give thanks in all circumstances.**

Commissioning

ONE: Give thanks continually to the God who loves you.

ALL: **Thanks to God who is the source of life.**
Thanks to God who is the sustainer of all living things.

ONE: Give thanks to God continually.

ALL: **Thanks for the good memories of life in past days.**
Thanks for all that is good in the present.

ONE: Give thanks to God continually.

ALL: **Thanks for the blessings found in faithful community.**
Thanks for the blessings found in family and with friends.

ONE: Give thanks continually.

ALL: **Thanks for patience in our struggles.**
Thanks for hope in our dark moments.

ONE: Give thanks to God continually,

ALL: **for our thanksgiving will never be done.**

All Saints' Day

November 1, or 1st Sunday in November

Daniel 7:1–3, 15–18
Psalm 149
Ephesians 1:11–23
Luke 6:20–31

Jesus talks about happiness and sorrow and encourages the love of enemies

Call to Worship

ONE: Rejoice! You worship in the company of the present-day saints.

ALL: **We are glad we worship with our friends.**

ONE: Rejoice! You worship in the tradition of the saints.

ALL: **We are glad we worship where faithful men and women have worshiped and served in years gone by.**

ONE: Rejoice! You worship remembering those who have witnessed to Christ in their living and in their dying.

ALL: **We are glad we have the example of the apostle Paul, Francis of Assisi, Martin Luther King Jr., Mother Theresa, and Oscar Romero to inspire us.**

ONE: Rejoice! You are the saints of this faith community and this generation.

ALL: **We are glad that we have been called to the compassionate work of Jesus Christ in this church and neighbourhood.**

Opening Prayer

ONE: Loving God, striving to keep your creation good,

ALL: **we are about your vital work.**

ONE: Loving God, ready to speak out for the way of Jesus Christ,

ALL: **we are your faithful people.**

ONE: Loving God, rejoicing that we can serve with others in the faith community,

ALL: **we find fulfilment.**

ONE: Loving God, prepared to confront the powers and systems of our time,

ALL: **we are challenged.**

ONE: Strengthen us, encourage us, inspire us, and stay with us, most loving God. Amen.

A Saints Prayer *(remembering that saints are not perfect)*

ONE: Like Peter the apostle, we recognize that we let fear hinder us.

ALL: **Free us to serve faithfully, Holy One.**

ONE: Like Jerome, we welcome criticism until it is directed at us.

ALL: **Free us to listen to the truth, Holy One.**

ONE: Like Thomas Merton, we can be short-tempered and impatient.

ALL: **Free us to be patient and compassionate, Holy One.**

ONE: Like Patrick of Ireland we can hold on to a grudge.

ALL: **Free us to leave the past in the past, Holy One.** *(time of silent reflection)*

Assurance of God's Concern

ONE: God does not call us to be perfect.
God calls us to rejoice in those gifts and talents we use generously and hopefully.

ALL: **God calls us to look honestly and thoroughly at our life's pattern, and to make the direction changes that are necessary.** *(time of silent reflection)*

ONE: God will give us pardon, peace, and courage for a new way.
God encourages us to look to the shortcomings of our nation and its leaders, and to consider by what actions, small or large, we can bring change.

ALL: **God cares about climate change, about the plight of refugees, about children who are forced work, and about the unequal use of limited global resources.** *(time of silent reflection)*

ONE: God will go with you as you play your part in compassionate and just work for change. Amen.

Offering Prayer

ONE: Give as the saints give and gave.

ALL: **We will give after reflection and prayer.**
       We will give with compassion to those we know.
       We will give with compassion to those whose needs we know.
       We will give with generosity; we will give sacrificially.
       We will give to support those in the faith community.
       We will give to support those in our neighbourhood and far beyond.

One   And God will bless your giving.

ALL: **Amen.**

Pastoral Prayer Pattern

ONE: A call from Jesus, a call from the saints of past time, a call from the saints of our time:

ALL: **love your enemies.**

ONE: Even in countries where corruption means that few get excellent health care and the vast majority get little,

ALL: **love your enemies.**

ONE: Even when long waiting lists are symbols of healing seriously delayed,

ALL: **love your enemies.**

ONE: Even when good friends have let you down and family members have spoken harsh words,

ALL: **love your enemies,**

ONE: Even when there are those who advise you to stop grieving,

ALL: **love your enemies.**

ONE: A call from Jesus, a call from the saints of past time, a call from the saints of our time:

ALL: **love your enemies.**

ONE: A call from Jesus, a call from the saints of past time, a call from the saints of our time:

ALL: **love your enemies.**

ONE: Even when you cannot forget a crushing remark,

ALL: **love your enemies,**

ONE: Even when your trust has been betrayed,

ALL: **love your enemies.**

ONE: Even when your most cherished dream has been dashed,

ALL: **love your enemies.**

ONE: Even when your life of faith has been belittled, love your enemies,

ALL: **and work and dialogue and protest and pray that change will become reality and suffering will be relieved.**

Commissioning *(from Luke 6:20–23)*

ONE: Who are the saints helping today?

ALL: **They are helping those who are poor – poor because they cannot buy or rent what they need.**

ONE: Who are the saints helping today?

ALL: **They are helping the hungry – hungry in a world where food is wasted every day.**

ONE: Who are the saints helping today?

ALL: **They are helping those who have suffered loss – loss of work, loss of self-esteem, loss of a friend or life partner.**

ONE: Who are the saints helping today?

ALL: **They are helping the rejected and the voiceless, the oppressed and ignored.**

ONE: Are you ready to claim your sainthood?

Memorial/Remembrance/ Veterans' Sunday

Call to Worship

ONE: We will remember those who faithfully went to war. They fought hard; some were injured and some died.

ALL: **We will remember them.**

ONE: We will remember members of the armed forces, their families, and those who support them.

ALL: **We will remember them.**

ONE: We will remember innocent civilians, children and adults who were caught up in the conflict.

ALL: **We will remember them.**

ONE: We will remember those who today are caught up in warfare, and refugees who have had to run for their lives.

ALL: **We will remember them.**

Opening Prayer

ONE: We strive for freedom of thought and word and action,

ALL: **and we give thanks for those who fought to preserve freedom.**

ONE: Where there is apathy,

ALL: **we will counter it with action.**

ONE: Where there is prejudice,

ALL: **we will speak out for equal opportunity.**

ONE: Where there is injustice,

ALL: **we will insist on the just way.**

ONE: Where there are barriers to moving forward,

ALL: **we will speak and act to bring the barriers down.**

ONE: As we give thanks for those who kept us free,

ALL: **so we pledge ourselves to be freedom-bringers. Amen.**

A Prayer of Sacrifice

ONE: On the cross, Jesus gave up his life.

ALL: **It would have been so much easier to avoid conflict with the powerful.**

ONE: On the cross, Jesus gave up his life.

ALL: **It would have been so much easier to forget his faithful principles.**

ONE: On the cross, Jesus gave up his life.

ALL: **His friends gave in to their self-concerns and their fears.**

ONE: On the cross, Jesus gave up his life,

ALL: **and was seen as just another mistaken follower of the one true God.**

ONE: What are we called to sacrifice? *(time of silent reflection)*

Assurance of God's Peace in the Struggle

ONE: We struggle with the right choices,

ALL: **and you, loving God, give us the resolve we need.**

ONE: We struggle to live faithful to the pattern of Jesus,

ALL: **and you, loving God, enable us to see the Jesus way.**

ONE: We struggle to share love with our family and friends,

ALL: **and you, loving God, are with us as we walk the extra mile.**

ONE: It is tough to keep on struggling, but you, loving God, have given us the promise of peace;

ALL: **peace in the struggle and peace when our struggling is done for good. Amen.**

Offering Prayer

ONE: We give so little, when others have given everything.

ALL: **Receive and bless our gifts, loving God, and use them to bring peace where there is conflict, and hope where the outlook is dismal and despairing.**

ONE: We pray in the name of Jesus, the peace-bringer, in the name of Jesus the peace-sustainer.

ALL: **Amen.**

Pastoral Prayer Pattern

ONE: As those who have seen the effect of conflict,

ALL: **we will work for peace.**

ONE: Loving God, we pray for those who are in conflict zones, and for those who are training to fight.
We pray for those imprisoned by warring factions, and for those who are running for safety.
We pray for refugees in Lebanon, Syria, and Turkey.
We pray for those who work to prevent terror attacks, and for those who talk with terrorists.
We pray for the mediators and the peacemakers, and for all who strive to end war.
As those who have seen the effects of conflict,

ALL: **we will work for peace.**

ONE: As those who have seen the effect of conflict,

ALL: **we will work for peace.**

ONE: We pray for those who promote the cause of peace within the local congregations, including (*specific local situation*)
We pray for those who foster the cause of refugees.
We pray for those agencies that help those who have been injured in conflict.
We pray for those who protest war peacefully.
We pray for world leaders who are active peacemakers.
As those who have seen the effect of conflict,

ALL: **we will work for peace.**

Commissioning

ONE: Go from here as those who will not forget.

ALL: **We go remembering the sacrifice made by young men and women striving to counter hatred and the abuse of power.**
We go remembering the loss of human life and poten-

tial in two world wars and conflicts beyond.
We go remembering those who have been injured in
conflict and who still suffer.
We go remembering civilians who have been injured in
mind and body because of war, and we remember
those who care for them.

ONE: Will you forget?

ALL: **We will not forget.**

Other Service Prayers

Prayers for Use before the Readings

ONE: Prepare to hear God's Word.

ALL: **We rejoice that scripture still speaks in telling ways.**

ONE: Be still and know that God is with you.

ALL: **We rejoice that God is also with us in the silence.** *(time of silent reflection)*

ONE: Know that we will be called to act on what we hear.

ALL: **We rejoice that we can bring change for God for good.**

     ***

ONE: Listen deeply for God's Word in the *prophesies/words of Paul/stories of Jesus,* and you will be aware of your call to discipleship.

ALL: **We will listen, we will reflect, and we will follow faithfully. Amen.**

     ***

ONE: Loving God, you are with us today as we hear your Word and as we respond to your call to action. Amen.

     ***

ONE: As we hear the scriptures two questions arise:

ALL: **What is God's intention? What is our response?**

     ***

ONE: As we listen deeply to the reading, as we reflect on what we hear,

ALL: **there will be understanding. There will be challenge. We will respond. Amen**

Before the Readings – Advent

ONE: As we prepare for the coming of Jesus we listen to these *joyful/peaceful/hopeful/loving* words,

ALL: **and we give God heart-full thanks. Amen.**

Before the Readings – Christmas

ONE: Wonderful God, these familiar stories of the birth of Jesus have a message for "all who have ears to hear."

ALL: **We will listen, we will celebrate, and we will live as those who know that God's anointed one is here. Amen.**

Before the Readings – Epiphany

ONE: Loving God, your Word is a light for us in a dark world.

ALL: **We have insight for our challenged times.**
      We have compassion when disaster strikes.
      We have community when sharing is called for.
      Loving God, we will reflect your light. Amen.

Before the Readings – Lent

ONE: These are words that speak of the commitment of Jesus.

ALL: **We are thankful.**

ONE: These are words that speak of the testing of Jesus.

ALL: **We are challenged.**
      These are words that speak of the suffering of Jesus.

ALL: We are called to compassion. Amen.

Before the Readings – Easter

ONE: Loving God, your risen Word brings us to life from death. Alleluia! Amen.

Before the Readings – Pentecost Sunday

ONE: Holy Spirit, you bring us together to celebrate the birthday of the church, the holy time of Pentecost.

ALL: **As we hear the words of scripture, touch us and hold us. As we reflect on those words, move us and inspire us. As we come to commitment in those words, strengthen us and encourage us to make a faithful and practical response. Amen.**

Prayers for after the Scripture Reading and before the Sermon

ONE: May the words that I speak and the reflection that we all share find a response that is worthy of you, most just, most loving, and most compassionate God. Amen

***

ONE: Join with us, living God, as we meet around your Word and reflect upon it.

ALL: **Encourage us. Inspire us. Put us to work. Amen.**

***

ONE: You have heard the Word for today.

ALL: **We are ready to take to heart a word for us and for our faith community.**

ONE: I am ready to reflect on the Word.

ALL: **We are ready to listen and to act. Amen.**

***

ONE: The reading of scripture is over.

ALL: **God's Word has become our words, and now the hard work begins.**

ONE: We will search for God's way for our time.

ALL: **We will search for a way that is compassionate:**

ONE: God's way.

ALL: **We will search for a way that has love at the centre:**

ONE: God's way.

ALL: **We will search for faithful fellow travellers:**

ONE: God's way.

ALL: **We will search for patience in the struggle:**

ONE: God's way.

ALL: **We will find peace along the way. Amen.**

***

ALL: **Living God, written in bygone ages but still relevant, heard by countless saints of the faith but still a life-changing witness,**
your Word finds us,
your Word tests us,
your Word inspires us,
your Word motivates us.
For your Word we thank you, living God. Amen.

Before the Sermon – Advent, John the Baptist

ONE: Loving God, give us the grace to hear some hard words, as well as the warm and easy words, this Advent.

ALL: **We are ready to begin the turnaround. Amen**

Before the Sermon – Passion

ONE: The cross words cause us to stop and look up.

ALL: **The cross words cause us to question our commitment.**

ONE: The cross words cause us to question people of power.

ALL: **The cross words cause us to renew our courage.**

ONE: I will reflect on the cross words,

ALL: **and we will listen carefully. Amen.**

Before the Sermon – Easter

ONE: It is old news, it is new news: "Jesus is risen!"

ALL: **We will rejoice, for we hear it as if for the very first time.**
Thanks be to God! Amen.

Before the Sermon – Pentecost

ONE: Your Spirit calls us, O God.

ALL: **Your Spirit inspires us, leads us on, enlivens us, calls us to action, and we give thanks. Amen.**

Hebrew Scripture Index

New Testament Scripture Index

Wood Lake

Imagining, living and telling the faith story.

WOOD LAKE IS THE FAITH STORY COMPANY.

It has told:
• The story of the seasons of the earth, the people of God, and the place and purpose of faith in the world
• The story of the faith journey, from birth to death
• The story of Jesus and the churches that carry his message.

Wood Lake has been telling stories for more than 35 years. During that time, it has given form and substance to the words, songs, pictures and ideas of hundreds of storytellers.

Those stories have taken a multitude of forms – parables, poems, drawings, prayers, epiphanies, songs, books, paintings, hymns, curricula – all driven by a common mission of serving those on the faith journey.

Wood Lake Publishing Inc.
485 Beaver Lake Road
Kelowna, BC, Canada V4V 1S5
250.766.2778

www.woodlake.com